Truly Human

Barbara Bacigalupi

Requests for permission to make copies of any part of the work should be mailed to:

Permissions Department, UMANO Inc.
442 Post Street, Second Floor, San Francisco, CA 94102
Tel.: (415) 989-9850 Fax: (415) 989-9854
E-mail: copyrights@umano.com

Ordering Information

Individual sales. UMANO publications, music, audiobooks, and other products can be ordered on the World Wide Web at www.umano.com; by telephone or fax at the numbers above; or by mail to the address above, attn: Sales Department.

Quantity sales. Special discounts are available on quantity purchases by corporations, associations, educational institutions and others. For details, contact the Sales Department at the address above.

Cover design: Barbara Bacigalupi
Interior design: Sarah Jane Charubin & Lenora Shishido
Illustrations: Sarah Jane Charubin
Editorial: Gary Schmidt & Lenora Shishido
Printing: Madison Street Press, Oakland, CA
Photo credits: Pete Carmichael, Sarasota, FL (xiii, 76, 80-88, 91-98, 100, 102, 104, 106, 108, 113, 171)
Judy Houston, Hayward, CA (173, 178)
Russell Baer, Santa Monica, CA (176)

ISBN: 1-893470-00-8
Library of Congress Catalog Card Number: 99-070794
First edition
Printed on acid-free recycled paper in the United States of America.

For my parents

Aileen and Robert Bacigalupi,
who have unconditionally loved me
and who have been with me
not only during the joys of my life,
but also throughout
my personal trial by fire.

Contents

LETTER TO MY READERS

At the very start of this book I want you to know I have but one goal for you — and that is:

I sincerely want you to be successful.

Not through a brief moment of fame or fortune, nor through quick fix, luck-of-the-draw victories. Rather, the success I am speaking of is genuine, and so grows continuously over the course of a distinctly human and uniquely gifted lifetime.

Please allow me to introduce myself to you as a strategic planning consultant. I have been privileged throughout my career to work with those who have dedicated themselves to the service of others, as members of the professions of medicine, health care, law, accounting, environmental consulting, ministry, and education.

These professionals represent the epitome of our founding fathers' American dream, and every parent's hope for their children. After all, our country's premise is that in an environment of freedom and justice, a good education — combined with courage and a lasting commitment to hard work — will grant each of us "life, liberty, and the pursuit of happiness."

The people I have come to know during the course of my consulting are the hearts, minds, and hands of their organizations. They have taught me much by allowing me to support their efforts in the face of enormous challenge and change. Now I wish to share with you what I have learned from them — and from my own personal experiences — about what is essential for human success.

What I will bring you in *Truly Human* is an introduction to the strategic visioning of human life. I have formulated this book's content in response to what I have observed as the barrier that most frequently prevents clients from achieving their professional and personal best. Because this pivotal issue centers on the need to acquire skills and experience in visioning, rather than the development of plans, I will focus here on *vision*.

Fortunately, strategic visioning is a process, and so each of us can build expertise by learning and practicing its component techniques. While everyone is able to vision, those of us who have access to proven methods are more likely to minimize risk and to achieve and perpetuate authentic success throughout our lives.

My mission is to give you access to visioning techniques, so you can avoid the trial and error of attempting to figure out the process on your own. For envisioning all you can become, and then planning an optimistic future that brings this vision into reality, is exercising the very essence of your humanity.

In *Truly Human*, I will concentrate on ways to enable you to envision your success in life as a continuous, self-directed process. Utilizing a metaphor of authentic growth drawn from nature, I can help you to meet each and every new day with greater personal integrity, courage, and intention.

This book is written for everyone; you don't need a professional license, or even a college degree, to benefit from the information I am about to present. That is because every individual, by virtue of being human, is endowed with the ability to envision the future and then strategically plan how to make this future a reality.

As you read through this book, it is important for you to understand my specific consulting philosophy. It is my belief that I am not here to make decisions for you. I am sure you know all too well, as do I, what it is like to have people tell you how you should live your life. But the truth is that *no one but you* can presume to know what is best for you. And so my approach is in sharp contrast to those who might try to convince you that their expectations are right for you.

Accordingly, the ideas and viewpoints I will present here are not intended to be taken as dogma, mandates, or rules that you should automatically accept as truth and follow blindly. Rather, I encourage and expect you to think each issue through carefully. Think wide and deep. Engage all your wisdom, feelings, and desires, for it is only through purposeful thinking that you will discover your unique vision in life.

I am simply here to create an environment in which you can gain a more complete understanding of what it means for you to be a *truly human* human being. I will raise many questions throughout the text. Use them to trigger your thinking. You may find it helpful to take notes and jot down your reflections along the way. Make this book your own, returning to it again and again as your life circumstances change.

To achieve the greatest benefit from this book, it is best to read the content through in sequence. This is because I have designed the issues so that each builds upon what has been said previously. Take each issue presented *personally*. That is, infuse each topic with the specifics of *your life*. Take careful notice of how your emotions and reactions change through the course of your reading. These self-measurements will stimulate your intuition and deepen your understanding of the subject matter.

To be quite honest, you may experience frustration with some of the issues presented, but do not allow this feeling to deter you from moving forward. Frustration is a phase you will most likely need to pass through as a means for increasing authentic success.

If you choose to make it happen, the journey presented in *Truly Human* will forever cause you to think in new and powerful ways about yourself. So let the joy and work of being truly human begin.

Best regards,
Barbara Bacigalupi
San Francisco, California

Nature provides clues that help us discover
the essence of our humanity.

PART ONE

AN

OPENING

REFLECTION

CONSIDER
YESTERDAY

What exactly does yesterday — this one day out of all the days of your life — look like to you?

What are the sounds, feelings, smells, and tastes you remember as you move through the minutes and hours, beginning with your first conscious moment, right through to the last thought that filled your mind before drifting off to sleep?

Give yourself permission to slow down the speed of your instant replay camera — not just a bit, but so that your actions take on the characteristics of slow-motion photography. Now, with every aspect of life portrayed as an exaggeration, you can more easily look beyond the extraneous motions of daily life to see what is really happening.

As you proceed, notice if certain feelings arise inside you. Can you identify specific emotions as you recall every moment of your day? Or do you find that you are mostly passive, feeling very little at all?

How much of this day was structured and procedurized? Estimate a percentage of your total

waking time given to these mechanized and repetitive activities. Of this percentage, how much was by your own choice and purposeful planning, and how much reflected the decisions of others about how they expect you to spend your day?

3

Did this day fit into a greater design that you have formulated for the course of your entire life? At day's end, how much closer were you to the fulfillment of your ambitions and dreams? How much nearer were you to achieving the goals that define the destiny and purpose of your life?

What went on inside your head at the end of the day? Was there peace? Did a sense of well-being flow easily from the knowledge that you did something good with this day, and that what you did was done well — performed with quality, even with an eye toward excellence?

Or was the feeling queasy and unsettled, as if the energy had been drained from every limb following your daylong struggle with time and with those around you? How many of your thoughts, as you tried to find restful sleep, focused on what was left undone — and on how much more will still wait to be accomplished tomorrow?

How much frustration has built inside you from the regret of not having spent this one most precious day— one you will never get another chance at — on something better? Something with more substance and meaning? Something that you can take deep pride in having accomplished well?

Now consider the days of your week, the weeks of your months, the months of your years.

What are the odds that you will reach your life goals if things stay as they are right now?

Are you satisfied with the present as the primary predictor of how your future will look and feel? Will the underpinnings of today facilitate a tomorrow that is rich with all you want and deserve? If you can sincerely respond "yes," then close this book now. Just continue on your life's journey, but always stay vigilant to why you have achieved your current success in life so that this success can be perpetuated over the course of an entire lifetime.

But if your answer is anything less than an unqualified and resounding "yes," you are, to some extent, caught up in the robotic mold of modern living. Too much of yesterday was dreary, monotonous — even lifeless. Today is just the same, each moment vanishing into the next, each day a mirror image of the one before as you forcibly drive yourself through the tedium of the world that surrounds you. Your days are crammed full of activities and obligations, but you are numb to their full results and consequences.

Keep this pattern up and there's one outcome you can count on — a paralysis that will likely make you vulnerable to crisis. What was once reserved for mid-life can now be yours at any age, if you have allowed mindless repetition to lull you into the sleep of those who live life on autopilot. All that's needed is a trigger, an unexpected event that throws you out of sync with the rhythm of life — and much of your precious time and energy will be spent putting your life back on track.

Longevity and prosperity are certainly ideals worth striving for. But now that we are living very long lives, how often is the prosperity portion of the equation achieved? We may achieve it in terms of dollars and cents, but what about the personal prosperity that flows from a life built on continuous growth toward our full and unique human potential?

We work harder and harder. We strive to fill each moment of each and every day with tangible and enduring results.

But *do your days add up to steady progress toward your definition of lifelong prosperity?*

Or do you find that you just have more meaningless days that don't fit into a purposeful context? Day after day of a long life that doesn't offer much more than an increased likelihood of shutting down your dreams and feelings?

How many stalls, breaks, and storms can you successfully weather?

We have come to believe so much in this modern way of life that the life crisis is now both anticipated and worn as a badge of honor — a pseudo-achievement that stands in the place of authentic living. Still, it's a fact that sooner or later most of us find ourselves living in the crisis mode, each day's pressures having far more control over us than we have over them.

This is no way to live!

You can't be truly human without realizing that there simply has to be a better way to mark the passage of each day. After all, a fresh approach, even a simple change of viewpoint and perspective, may allow you to live closer to your authentic self each and every day of your life.

PART TWO

THE

TIME

CONSPIRACY

NATURE'S RHYTHM

No matter how much we might like to suspend time — to catch up with ourselves, our work, our families and friends — there's no stopping the world from moving forward. Whether we like it or not, once our lives are set in motion, each day follows the previous one for as many days as we inhabit our physical bodies.

There's no getting around the fact that for the here and now of living, the worlds around us and inside us are programmed with rhythms. These rhythms constitute an organic flow of forward movement that serves to continually remind us of the passage of time. We humans, like all living creatures, are innately attuned to nature's masterful timekeeping system, which provides us with the security of knowing that day follows night, follows day, follows night, and so on.

Tides move toward shore only to recede into themselves again. The moon slivers, then rounds itself out again with the light of the sun. We're literally surrounded by a symphony of well-orchestrated

rhythms that soothe and reassure us that there will be a future waiting for us.

Yet within this repetitive structure, there is also variation. The proportion of light to darkness varies throughout the 365-day countdown we have chosen to call a year. The seasons change, taking us from winter's cold to summer's warmth; from autumn's aging to spring's rebirth.

Nature's method for measuring time facilitates our awareness of our own human experience, as we progress from birth to physical maturity, through inner growth, and eventually to physical death.

Wherever we go, nature's timekeeping system is ever present to us, working from the inside out and the outside in, constantly urging us on to ... well, that's the crux of the matter. We are being urged toward a blank space, a void, a line without words, a path without directional signs — and that is the real challenge of being alive.

"Fill the void that time creates" is the mandate given to all living things. And that is easy to accomplish if you are a bacterium, or a garden snail, or a rhinoceros. Just follow your instincts; millions of years of trial-and-error experiments in the evolutionary process have made you ever more fit for the task at hand. The odds are on your side that instinct will lead you to successfully find food and shelter, avoiding predators and competitors in order to reach maturity, reproduce, and perpetuate the species.

But as members of *Homo sapiens,* we are blessed with an enormous capacity for consciousness. In the late 1960's, when I first encountered *The Phenomenon of Man,* written by the noted twentieth century anthropologist and philosopher Pierre Teilhard de Chardin, I became fascinated by the scope and implications of consciousness. Teilhard de Chardin's thinking helped me begin a personal journey, one which attempts to differentiate the state of knowing from one in which I am *aware of what I know.* He pointed to our awesome ability as humans to live beyond the confines of pure instinct, empowered by the wisdom from all the information and experiences we have drawn from our surrounding world.

We all have an inner life — a spirit, a soul — that allows us to make decisions. And nature has left it up to each of us to make *meaningful, conscious* decisions about how we spend each day, each month, each year. So why do we routinely encounter dissatisfaction as we reflect on the content of our days?

Be honest with yourself.

Are you consciously deciding how you fill the time in your life?

MECHANIZING TIME

hy, then, in the midst of nature's ingenious design, do we tolerate living even one day — let alone a lifetime — with dissatisfaction as our frustrating companion? If the power to change is ours by virtue of heightened consciousness, then what makes us willing to tolerate days without substance and meaning? After all, life on autopilot is a dehumanizing option.

The reason I was able to verbalize the sentiments expressed in the opening reflection is that my own life has been affected by such feelings and circumstances. Because you have chosen to open this book, you, too, probably share in these same reactions to a less-than-fulfilling daily life. This also tells me that you sincerely desire a better outcome. Yet something may be holding you back from making the essential changes that will replace your discontent with lasting satisfaction.

Stop for a moment to consider yourself as a human being. Do you desire the fulfillment of your goals and dreams? If your dreams still seem miles away, maybe even out of sight, there have to be some very good reasons why are you settling for less than you deserve.

So let us together ask why we tolerate feelings of powerlessness, even despair. Why do we put up with life as it is, as opposed to how it could be? If something is preventing us from fully pursuing our conscious humanity, no time can be wasted in getting to the heart of what stands between us and our authentic and ultimate success.

Let us begin by examining our mind-set toward time. Nature already provides an organic flow that allows us to benchmark our progress, facilitating an awareness of past experience and present circumstances. This wisdom, when combined with our ability to draw insights about our best options for the future, should make us masters of the time of our lives — not its slaves.

Is it possible that we have been unable to accept the inherent simplicity in nature's design? The clock is, after all, human-made, not part of nature. Ever since its introduction, we humans have inaugurated a process for counting time in smaller and smaller increments that has continued to the present. As we superimposed our mechanical time-keeping devices over nature's rhythm, our increasing technological capabilities allowed us to split days into hours, then hours into minutes, minutes into seconds, and seconds into nanoseconds.

It now seems as though each fraction of time conspires with the next and the next and the next, always confronting us with the tick-tock of the clock — a clock which we have given gargantuan hands that can reach out and hold us hostage. Our perception of time has moved away from nature's inherent, reassuring promise of tomorrow, to that of an overbearing monster that dogs our days and nights. In short, time has become an enemy instead of a friend. And we are the ones responsible for setting this adversarial relationship in place.

Mere knowledge of our love affair with mechanized time-splitting devices is probably insufficient to free us from the dissatisfaction of everyday life. So we need to examine *why and how* we became so willing to displace nature's rhythms with the tyranny of these artificial timekeepers. For with greater awareness of what we know, we may make more inspired decisions about our daily relationship with the time of our lives.

FILLING
THE
VOID

When faced with a challenge to heighten my own consciousness, I seek out the arts in order to create a contrast to my daily routine. This is how I open myself to new insights. After all, it is the privilege of artists to confront us with ourselves and what we have done with our world.

The most effective artists are those whose statements are made so vigorously that we are compelled to react — to rethink who we are, what we stand for, and where we have come from. Once artists help me achieve this perspective of heightened awareness, I find that I can decide where to go and how best to get there with greater ease, confidence, and overall likelihood of success.

And so, while sitting in New York City's new Ford Center for the Performing Arts, watching *Ragtime — The Musical's* representation of E. L. Doctorow's best-selling novel, I gained a powerful clue to how our obsession with time came into being. There on the stage, fact and fiction combined to show how American immigrants from vastly different cultures, values, and capabilities came together to forge a new society in the early 1900s. The tensions and issues of that era were depicted right before my eyes in such compelling images that the present was temporarily blocked from my mind. The actors were so adept, and so committed to taking me with them on this larger-than-life re-creation of our American industrial age, that surrender was easy.

I could not escape feeling the rising intensity of my own emotions as this vision of life at the dawn of the twentieth century unfolded. This was what life had been like for my grandparents and great-grandparents; and for three hours, the lifestyle they had experienced became mine, too.

At the center of the story was a car — and the ensuing battle between those who owned it and those who coveted it. Not just any car, mind you, but a shiny black and glistening chrome Model-T Ford that was envied by all who saw it.

As *Ragtime* proceeded to unfold its unfor-gettable message in the very theater that Ford Motor Company had helped to build, Henry Ford himself appeared, resurrected from the afterlife. High above the stage on a cold steel transom, the Model-T's inventor spoke with pride of his inven-tion, a method of production that would soon allow everyone to be able to possess one of these automobiles. For he had found the "secret" to making many, many more in a fraction of the time it had taken to build the first.

16   Below the transom and across the back of the dimly lit stage was Henry Ford's secret solution — an assembly line, powered by nameless, faceless human beings, each applying their muscle to accomplish the tedious task of turning bolt after bolt to manufacture many more automobiles just as bright and shiny as the first.

      The repetitive motion of each person on the line — their hands holding each bolt in exactly the same place, moving in exactly the same way to rotate each bolt precisely the same amount — soon blurred, so that the people became indistinguishable from the bolts they turned. But the glue that melded both bolt and bolt-turner into one efficient unit was never what attracted the workers to the task. It was the dream that this work would provide the steady salary that over time would allow them to afford one of the same Model-T's they now assembled.

      People and bolts, bolts and people, all serving to fill time to capacity. A tighter bolt with every tick-tock of the factory's clock. Industrial-age success courtesy of Henry Ford — and all the titans of corporate America who followed in his footsteps.

Ragtime made a most powerful case that the results of these achievements in the first half of the twentieth century constituted a distinct point of transformation in the history of humankind. While not quite as revolutionary as when, millions of years ago, our first ancestors used their uniquely adept opposable thumbs to grasp what would become tools for manual labor, these gains proved so profound that there would be no turning back. The benefits of steady income, a car, and a home were too good to pass up, especially after years of sacrifice during depression and war.

An entirely new way of life emerged as a consequence, one that equates human accomplishment with the kind of *doing* that results in a tangible product that can be seen and touched.

But what if this single-minded focus on *doing to make products* has helped seduce us away from the essential human form of doing — through heightened consciousness — that occurs inside our minds and souls? How well do our inner lives flourish in the midst of time-driven mass production?

TIME-CRAMMING

*B*ecause producing more per unit of time leads to a secure, quality standard of living, we have transformed productivity at work into a nationalized lifestyle goal. Our society has become so adept in the tactics of productivity that its concepts are now embedded in all facets of our modern American way of life. And to a point, this works quite well, so well that no matter what you do for a living, you are probably incorporating the tenets of productivity — now called time management — into your day.

Do you batch phone calls, so that you won't be constantly interrupted from planned activities and have to pay the price of starting and stopping tasks over and over again in midstream?

Do you group errands by location, hoping to reduce the total time involved?

Do you divide in order to conquer, each family member taking on a different chore in hopes that there will be enough time left over for the family to get together as a real family?

Are you skilled in the basics of time management? If not, you need to learn these techniques so that you can better organize the time available to you during each precious day.

Sooner or later, no matter how organized and time-aware you are, you will eventually reach a point of diminishing returns when time management becomes what I like to call *time-cramming* — a point when shortcuts can no longer be found. No more time can be saved because no more time is available. The only realistic option is to eliminate the least important activities altogether in order to restore balance to your days.

But this usually doesn't happen, and for good reason: when do we even have time to evaluate the relative importance of each activity amidst the confusion of so much doing? How can we find the space amidst mindless busyness to make quality decisions about how we spend our time? Too quickly we abandon our search for answers, and just keep doing.

Only here's the rub. The ultimate consequence of time-cramming is that we keep trying to do more, but in this maxed-out state *what we do is of lesser and lesser quality*. Even when spread too thin, we persist and attempt to boost total output. We adopt the notion that we can defy time, impervious to the effects time-cramming has on both our outer and inner selves. Like Henry Ford, we increase the speed of the assembly line to accelerate our progress in life.

Let's consider the consequences of this productivity-based decision.

20   Each day offers 24 hours for you to decide how to spend. If you sleep eight hours a night and work the average eight hours per day, you have eight hours left beyond sleep and work. That sounds like plenty of time for the rest of life's activities.

Now factor in the other basic personal activities you perform each day — commuting to and from work, personal hygiene and grooming, preparing and eating meals — and nearly half your discretionary time is now consumed.

But still, the business of daily life needs to be accounted for, including daily household chores, laundry, phone calls, reading mail, and paying bills. Time is running out. And if you exercise for 30 minutes, you might have, at best, two hours to accomplish everything else.

Interpersonal relationships, recreation, learning, watching TV or a movie, meeting a friend for coffee, surfing the Web, reading the newspaper or a book — all of these must somehow be crammed into the hour or two you have left. But what about your inner life? Is there room to reflect, meditate or pray for at least 30 minutes each day?

Now *here's where the trade-offs in your future quality of life really begin.*

You want to own a home, but a 50-hour workweek is necessary in order to earn an income level that qualifies for a mortgage. One way to solve this is to sacrifice one hour of sleep and one hour of your discretionary time per day.

21

Let's presume that you own this home of your dreams, and now would like to start a family. There are only 30 minutes of discretionary time available to raise your family, presuming you are willing to give up all TV, reading, recreation, personal growth activities, and so on.

Are 30 minutes *really enough time to raise and love your children?*

No, but you can make it work by giving up another hour or two of sleep every day for the next 18 years or more.

The bottom line of taking productivity too far isn't financial; rather, it is measured in terms of our ability to share ourselves with other human beings. Conversations become clipped and defined by what to do, where to go, and how to get there. It takes weeks to coordinate calendars for a simple lunch date. Once face to face, we impress each other with our daring accounts of doing and time-cramming. No wonder we find ourselves too often plagued by feelings of emptiness and superficiality when walking away from our encounters with others.

In this time-cramming scenario, what we are worth equals only what we do.

Self-worth is more often attached to how much tangible doing we accomplish. But self-worth, identity, and esteem are really intrinsic inner values which are confirmed by the presence of an inner life. When human value is equated solely with production, we devalue our innate worth as human beings.

If you are wondering how deeply time-cramming affects you, ask yourself these questions: Do feelings of self-doubt and insecurity creep into your thoughts when you allow yourself to stop doing? What quality of life remains in the midst of time-cramming? Are you at peace with yourself?

Only you can make this evaluation. Are you satisfied that you have sufficient time to THINK and FEEL? To build the TRUST that precedes nourishing relationships? To allow your HUMANITY to flourish? And if you are less than satisfied, are you ready to change?

What's next?

Let's move beyond the effects of time-cramming, to consider how standardization and procedure-driven work may hinder our inner growth.

PART THREE

BEYOND
THE TRIED
AND TRUE

THE DILEMMA
OF THE
PROFESSIONAL

While it may be possible to rationalize how the assembly line worker accepted mindless repetition in exchange for a secure standard of living, what happens at the opposite end of the career spectrum? To find out, let us explore what can happen to those who carry the title "professional."

Having served professionals in medicine, health care, accounting, law, education, and ministry over the past 15 years, my most serious observation is that these hardworking, dedicated people too often find themselves captive to productivity and to the standards that define their professions. What happens, as a result, to the professional's ability to generate ideas and give quality advice to others?

I believe that it is essential for all of us to understand the professional's dilemma. For as I will discuss later, *an information age requires each of us to take on the role and responsibilities of a professional.*

The professional's place in society.

By definition, a professional has studied long and hard to acquire a specialized base of knowledge and related skill set that benefits others. Because of this expertise and training, we hold professionals in high esteem, whether they be the surgeons who touch our hearts with their latex-gloved hands; the accountants who translate columns of numbers into financial health for multiple generations of a family; the engineers, architects, and contractors who make our freeways and skyscrapers safe; the ministers who guide spiritual growth from a pulpit; the educators who form the hearts and minds of our young people; or the attorneys who protect and defend us in our legal relationships with society.

We respect and believe in their desire and capability to help us. In fact, this dedication is at the very heart of what defines professionals, for they understand the trust others place in them. In turn, we value their advice, carefully weighing the meaning of each word they say, and knowing what powerful effects the professional can have on the quality and even the length of our lives.

The professional's responsibilities can facilitate personal growth.

Professional career paths not only benefit the people served, but also provide an excellent means for the professionals themselves to explore their own personal growth. What better way to develop one's humanity than to be trusted with such important decision making? There can be no doubt that the professional's daily work *demands* the heightened exercise of consciousness. Distinctly human thinking capabilities are part of the professional's daily routine. So what happens when professionals are forced to render service within the confines of productivity quotas and the bottom line?

26

Chargeable hours devalue ideas.

Given that we turn to professionals for expert ideas, in the form of advice, how do we compensate them? Ideas, by definition, cannot be measured against time. A solution can occur in a flash when two colleagues spend a couple of minutes in an office corridor talking over your special needs. Or it can take hours, days, or even weeks to germinate and eventually come to fruition.

Because an idea is hard to quantify, in terms of both value and time spent, we fall back on the old assembly line model when we compensate these professionals. While what we pay should be based on the value their advice and skills have on our lives, we instead count the minutes, the number of office visits, and we pay for the total *time* each professional spends working.

And so, we provide incentive to those who spend the most time writing the longest and wordiest documents, and who schedule the most frequent visits. In the end, the one who creates reasons for continuing consultation can receive greater reward than the effective professional who provides prompt and efficient resolution to your needs. This is indeed a situation of misplaced incentives.

If by chance you are an attorney, a public accountant, a doctor, or an engineer, you know all too well — as do I as a consultant — how the "chargeable hour" can negatively affect your work. *Doing* is what counts; generating ideas, learning, and researching too often go unrewarded.

By extension, we must consider what happens to you and me when we live in a society that diminishes the value of ideas. Just how often are you appreciated for your ideas — most of the time, occasionally, or so seldom that you can't really remember the last time your advice was requested? Most importantly, do you value yourself for your own ideas? I have encountered the response "I'm not an idea person" far too often. But if ideas are an intrinsic part of the very definition of humans as conscious beings, anything that diminishes the worth of an idea only serves to dehumanize us all.

The dilemma facing professionals can be complicated by their professional standards.

Each individual profession is defined by a specific set of standards of practice, ethics, a body of shared knowledge, and the mastery of a skill set. We as consumers depend on this definition to ensure that we receive service of a quality prescribed by the standards of the profession. But as with time-cramming, there is a point of diminishing returns when standards are taken so literally that they begin to limit the professional's ultimate success — which is the rendering of excellent quality service.

28

Even if you do not already carry a professional license, put yourself in the professional's place. Consider what might happen if you were confined to a narrowly defined scope of information and faced with frequent repetition of procedurized skills. Add to this the pressure to perform without error — a pressure well reinforced by your malpractice insurance premium — and leaps of thought and good ideas can easily seem like destructive and risky violations of what has already been proven to work.

In an environment requiring rigorous adherence to standards, it is no wonder why many of us accept *only the tried and true.*

THE
CHALLENGE

*N*ow imagine that that you live in a daily environment that upholds the tried and true, and that I arrive for a meeting as your personal strategic planning consultant. You have asked me to support you in creating a vision for the future. To your credit, you instinctively know that vision is necessary. Now when I ask you to describe this vision to me, just how easy will it be for you to respond?

Can you see *a future you* — someone who brings greater insight and understanding to daily life? In this vision, how different are your future days from today? What are you doing? What would you be thinking about? What effect would you have on others? Are you satisfied and happy?

Environment has great impact on our ability to create future vision.

Granted, your preliminary vision is fuzzy and tentative. But does it speak to the essence of who you are and who you can become? If you are to be genuinely successful in envisioning your future, what type of environment will best support you throughout this process? Will the regimen and focus of the tried-and-true mind-set help or hinder you? Will you be able to ask the tough questions that begin with the words "What if?"

30   The effects of productivity and time-cramming have reached well beyond the factory's time clock to permeate those career paths we revere for the complexity of thought and personal commitment required. If those very people who render advice and decisions for a living struggle with the creation of future vision, then none of us should be surprised to find that vision does not come easily. As you might surmise, I have concluded that the professional's dilemma of being too often bound to the tried and true just might be an endemic American problem.

Of course, there are always bright, outstanding professionals who stand out as hopeful exceptions to the norm. They reach well beyond average performance to that which is truly excellent. These individuals represent breakthrough thinking, going well beyond the tried and true to produce innovations and advances in their professions. They are the pioneers who create the future. They are responsible for pushing our age of productivity into one based on information.

So why are so many of us — from assembly line workers to professionals — incapable of the

breakthrough thinking that creates vision? Is it because only a few human beings are blessed with the gift of creating ideas? I think not. Rather, it all comes down to understanding how we have been constrained by productivity and time-cramming — and then motivating ourselves to learn the skills that will help us become all we are meant to be.

Future vision occurs within individuals.

Once I came to understand how ingrained our way of work was in all types of human endeavor, it became clear to me that the organizations I served would only be at their best when every individual was at his or her personal human best. For organizations and businesses are, by definition, groups of individuals who share in the same vision. As a result, the maturity level of each individual's capacity for envisioning the future determines the overall quality of vision formulated for an organization.

How can we ever use the benefits of heightened consciousness to create strategic visions for the future of our organizations if we cannot first access vision in our own individual lives?

Visionary people make visionary organizations, not the other way around. And we are all able to vision, even though a societal conspiracy seems to be working against our ability to build expertise in the *techniques* of vision.

Yet productivity cannot be abandoned.

While productivity, time-cramming, and adherence to the tried and true are in great part the roots of this conspiracy, don't jump to the conclusion that I am recommending a complete abandonment of our current way of doing, or that creating future vision requires individuals to drop out from mainstream society. Industrial-age productivity has been an absolutely essential stage in our human evolution. We cannot let go of these accomplishments, which have been successful in providing a quality of life that can support future vision. Instead, the *challenge* is for us to remain productive members of society — and to learn to use that productivity so that we are freed, rather than enslaved, by time. Our challenge is to bring the best attributes of productivity forward as facilitators, rather than enemies, of vision.

And we need to learn how to accomplish this in a new age that provides instant access to information, anywhere and at any time.

Are you ready for this challenge?

32

CHANGE
BEGINS
WITH FRUSTRATION

My first goal for you has been to surface and heighten the frustration daily life brings. For when we pause to think about it, change is nearly always motivated by frustration. And so, I quite deliberately designed this portrait of our American way of life to emphasize the *potential for harm* that exists in our productivity-dominated society.

I did this to demonstrate why many of us remain stuck in our current situations. Our time-cramming, mass-produced lifestyle makes us numb to the long-term effects of the present. By exaggerating the emptiness and dissatisfaction you may already experience at the end of your days, I hope you will better understand how this can happen.

If you are feeling frustrated right now, realize that this is substantive evidence that change is emerging within you. Congratulate yourself for beginning a process that will ultimately release your mind, your heart, and your soul.

To know how much change is needed, you will need to evaluate the depth and breadth of your frustration. Is it always there, nagging and persistent? Or is it intermittent and triggered only occasionally by changing life circumstances?

34 Intermittent frustration is a most powerful way to monitor when you can best make change proactively. In other words, you can use frustration constructively to alert yourself to the issues you must emphasize in your ongoing quest for personal growth. But while all the many manifestations of frustration require attention and action, it is the persistent, ever-present type which will most likely require a paradigm shift in how you view yourself and your place in the world. A state of constant frustration is not healthy for mind nor body.

Beyond frustration, you can also evaluate the extent to which your autopilot has taken over daily life. Have you ever driven home and then wondered how you got there? No need to think about the specific route you follow along the way; in effect, it has become so routine that you do not need to expend conscious effort. Quite similarly, we can go through the hours of our days without giving as much conscious attention as we might to the outcomes we achieve for ourselves. But waiting for us each night is the frustration of not having done something more meaningful with this precious day that we will never see again.

My intention throughout this book is to push you into a state of heightened awareness, so that you are better prepared to reach your own conclusions about how issues in our society are affecting you, and in turn, whether you will choose to make substantial and lasting change. Be aware that unless dissatisfaction with your current situation is persistent, change is highly unlikely. Now that you have completed the first step in this journey by surfacing your real frustrations, I am convinced that you will be able to fill your days with greater satisfaction.

Time and time again, I have observed how people who are motivated by good intentions attempt to be all things to all people. But in their daily quests against the clock, the quality of the long-term future is unnecessarily compromised. Adequate performance — "getting by" — substitutes for genuine excellence. But can you, as an individual, afford to settle for just getting by? What good will you be to yourself and others in this state of mind?

Instead, always rely on the strength of your human spirit to inspire you to strive for more — to want for yourself the security that stems from a well-envisioned future which leads you ever closer to your *truly human* self.

At this unique point in the history of humankind, standing between the industrial and information revolutions, what is the barrier that gets in the way of authentic, lasting success? It is the seductive nature of the status quo, which can delude us into thinking that our days fit like comfortable old shoes. For behind this comfort is a mind-set that lures us into believing that change will require more effort than it is worth. Add to this a view of the future as inherently dangerous and risky, and we can easily make seemingly rational arguments that keep us right where we are today.

36

If frustration with the present is the first step toward change, then a thorough understanding of the future is the second step. Change should never be taken lightly. Rather, it should be the wisest course of action or not ventured at all.

What's next?

An exploration of the wondrous benefits the future can hold for us when we seek out our truly human selves.

PART FOUR

A TRULY

HUMAN

VISION

BEING
TRULY
HUMAN

While the seeds of change are sown with frustration, their nurture requires a vision of what those seeds can grow to become. This is the vision each of us forms about our better self — the truly human person we seek to be in the future. We are only likely to deliberately introduce change into our lives if we wholeheartedly believe that the future will be significantly better than the present.

I have often attempted to reflect on this concept of a "future self." In the process, I have come to the realization that this reflective part of my personal journey — the understanding of my purpose in life — is best begun by understanding the purpose of human life itself.

What is the purpose of human life?

If we pause to consider how to go about finding our life's purpose, all we have to do is think about what other organisms do. The answer is quite simple: they GROW. In a universal sense, we too can define the purpose of our lives as the pursuit of growth. In doing so, we emphasize that growth is not an endpoint. Success is not determined by crossing a finish line; rather, it results from engaging continuously in a purposeful process. This applies whether an individual life is short or long. Being thoroughly immersed in growth is what matters most. Then, and only then, can a life be successful at any given point in time, for it is the process of growth that makes us whole.

What, then, is the basic accomplishment inherent to growth?

Once again, all we need do is look to nature for clues. Let's consider the tree as an example. When it grows, it *makes more of itself without changing its essential form or nature*. A tree is still a tree, but it becomes a tree of greater size — the circumference of its trunk expanding and making more, its height reaching taller and taller, its branches stretching further and further outward.

Making more — rather than making something totally different — is what growth is all about.

As I have already mentioned, heightened consciousness — the sheer magnitude of our ability to be aware of ourselves and all that we know — is the special gift we humans have been given in most generous proportion. Consciousness confers the rights, privileges, and consequences of decision making, and so allows us to expand our humanity. We are freed to move from the instinctive and preprogrammed to that which we choose on our own.

Who is in charge of our growth?

Here, in this state of hyperawareness, we are our own managers and leaders. As managers, we continually measure the effectiveness of past actions, using time as nature intended — as a benchmark to give perspective to lifetime progress. As leaders, we use past experience and knowledge of our current situation to create future vision and then plan sound alternative courses of action. Using logic and reason, we can identify the best way to achieve this vision. Hence, *heightened consciousness empowers us to self-direct our own growth.*

As a result of exercising our ability to decide where to go and how to get there, we become fully accountable for the consequences. Accordingly, we self-direct in ways that foster authentic growth.

When is growth authentic for the truly human human being?

This question goes to the heart of what constitutes membership in *Homo sapiens.* There are two major components of our humanity: that which is common to all members of our species, and those attributes that define each of us as individuals. Both aspects, if pursued fully, can allow us to reap the benefits of being *truly human* human beings.

40

What are the outcomes of our shared gift of heightened consciousness?

The same gift of consciousness that empowers us to self-direct also allows us to encounter ourselves and our world. And in the encounter, we experience life through our senses and react with our emotions. Our ability to stand upright and face the world with our minds and hearts open points to how specially prepared we are for this interaction with creation.

As we participate in creation, we make ideas out of the disconnected pieces of information and feelings we draw into our inner selves. While we may not be able to make something out of absolutely nothing, we are able to create our individual selves out of our unique nature and nurture.

How does our ability to create affect us?

If you create your future self through the interface of your unique giftedness with the distinct needs and wants of the surrounding world, no one but you can be you. No one else can possibly occupy your place in creation, experiencing and responding to life at the same time, in the same place, with exactly the same circumstances.

The pattern of personality traits, gifts, talents, and physical and intellectual abilities you have inherited is yours to develop and make your own. It is left to you to choose, at any given moment in the

course of your life, which abilities you will purposefully develop. The continuing evolution of your
truly human self will be unique in all of creation.
And so each of us, by virtue of this distinctive individuality, is prepared to make a significant, lasting
contribution to the world.

What happens to our inner creation?

Creativity does not exist in isolation. It
involves far more than ruminations within the mind,
or interior reflections of who we can become. To be
genuine, our inner life shares itself with others in
the world through acts of creation — actions that
live out our truly human decisions and intentions.

This is because we have been created to take
part in both a human and a universal community. I
believe that if we possess an ability, it is there for a
reason. We are meant to use what we are given. If
you ever doubt this for a moment, think of how
well your physical body has been prepared for
encountering your environment through your
senses — and then for communicating back with
your world using your advanced human capabilities
in language, mathematics, music, science, art, and
manual dexterity.

Through conscious action we are compelled
to share all that we are — the creative achievement
of our inner life — with others.

Why do we participate in communities?

Because each human being possesses these same capacities for sharing, we are both makers and beneficiaries of creative actions. Out of deep respect for these mutual capabilities, we can carry out our lives in affirmation of the essential human dignity and individuality in each of us.

We recognize that whenever growth is based on self-centered and narcissistic motivations, we may compromise each other by our less-than-generous actions. But if we inspire our growth with decisions that enhance the greater good, we will all become facilitators of our own and each other's success.

And so we desire to come together as truly human communities that achieve a synergy beyond the sum of individual contributions. For between us, we have not only all the necessary capabilities to respond to a world of changing circumstances, but also the courage to support and motivate each individual among us toward excellence.

You are absolutely necessary to creation. Your purposeful contribution to the world will always be uniquely yours, and your life experience will be like no one else's.

We grow in order to make more...

44   ...***more of our inner spirit/soul***...we recognize that our capacity for heightened consciousness allows us to self-direct our growth toward full ***potential***...

...***potential*** as a *truly human* human being...by creating ourselves as unique ***individuals***...

...***individuals*** who have an essential place and purpose in the world and so take part in ***community***...

...***community*** which respects the dignity inherent in all of ***creation.***

This is how I have gone about developing my definition of human growth. In creating this definition, I am also creating the core of my vision. These concepts must be present for the vision to be authentic. You can use this definition as the seed for your own vision of yourself. Later on in Part Seven, I will discuss the specific techniques you will need to use to develop your own vision.

Is this vision compelling?

Is *this vision of a truly human human being*
sufficiently compelling to motivate you to let go of
the status quo and embrace substantive change in
your life?

Are *you energized by childlike curiosity*, wondering what life would be like if you released the full
potential of your unique gifts and talents?

Do *you desire to immerse yourself fully in
all of creation*, knowing that you are well prepared
for whatever the future may bring?

Can *you feel the sense of excitement* that
comes with the creation of ideas, and in turn the creation of your truly human self?

Are *you ready* to commit to a life purpose
which centers on continuous growth as a *truly
human* human being?

Will *you allow yourself* to experience all that
the future holds for you?

THE BENEFITS
OF GROWTH

*T*he general vision I have attempted to portray of a *truly human* human being pales in comparison to the individual visions each of us is capable of seeing in our mind's eye. If we release our minds and hearts to see beyond the numbing status quo, we will not only begin to see our ultimate selves, but we will access the benefits of being truly human. Our lives will be better because of the tremendous results that flow to each of us when we are in a state of truly human growth. By making more of ourselves, we not only drive persistent dissatisfaction from our days, but we also reap the rewards of a job well done.

When I allow myself to think of what I can experience in this heightened state of awareness and self-directed development, these are the thoughts that come to *my* mind. What comes to yours?

As you proceed through my descriptions of the benefits I believe are associated with authentic growth, ask yourself how important each is to you. To what extent are these benefits already present in your life? What other benefits do you seek based on your unique nature and nurture? How does your present situation compare to the benefits that might be yours in the future?

Unless each of these benefits is well integrated into your life, there is still a need for change — a change from the status quo that will bring you an authentic way of life. After all, are you willing to settle for just a fraction of the total happiness you could achieve? By comparing the presence of these benefits today to what you desire in the future, you may gain insights into all that may be missing from your current daily life.

The Benefits of **TRULY HUMAN** Growth

Liberation of the **SPIRIT**

The growth of the spirit allows us to partake of our world more fully. We find the world surrounding us thoroughly irresistible   full of richness and variety. More and more of the world, and the entirety of creation, comes within the grasp of our minds. We are proud and confident in our original thoughts and ideas. We move from censoring and criticizing ourselves to taking sheer joy in our ability to think as far and wide, deep and high as we possibly can. Our horizons take on limitless proportions.

Inheritance of WISDOM

The experiences of those who have preceded us are available to enhance our own growing body of wisdom. We make greater strides because others have paved the way for us. But we do not incorporate the experiences of the past in ways that prevent us from making quality decisions based on today's environment. We take from the past only that which is relevant today. We move further in our development than could ever be achieved by using only what is tried and true.

Mid-life Crisis PREVENTION

The mid-life crisis is no longer expected to mark major life transitions or times of difficult circumstances. Instead, we see our lives from a greater vantage point that places everything in perspective. We are not victims. We are confident in our ability to react to change with ease and grace.

By anticipating change, we do not need to wear ourselves out — nor sacrifice our good health — in order to grant ourselves the permission to stop doing whatever it is that we do not like. Instead, we evaluate and identify sources of frustration as soon as they appear, and take action before situations spin out of control. We are less likely to seek out radical, disconnected solutions that may overwhelm and bring our progress in life to an abrupt halt. We can learn from everything life brings our way. Personal crisis is no longer our expected nor frequent companion.

Optimal HEALTH

Because of these benefits, we want to live a quality life for as long as possible. We replace the persistent, dangerous stress that comes from dissatisfaction with daily life with the optimistic viewpoint that future vision confers. We can readily access relaxation, and do so regularly to protect ourselves from stress-related illness and injury. This, in turn, extends quality health over a longer life.

We further seek to integrate the mind and body, and to understand the relationship of symptoms, genetic inheritance, and environment to our health. We make commitments to good health practices, including nutrition and exercise, that promote wellness and prevent disease. We feel and look our best, not in response to images portrayed by the media nor the expectations of others, but because we are in a continuing state of optimal health.

A World of OPPORTUNITIES

The world opens to us. It abounds with opportunities that we can use to catalyze our continuing personal growth. Natural vigilance characterizes

our relationship with all that surrounds us. We
understand how our talents are needed and how
opportunity challenges us to always be more. By
listening more carefully, by seeing beyond the
superficial, we take information and forge it into
the knowledge that guides our life-planning decisions. Our lives are relevant now and become ever
more relevant with the passage of time.

Evolving CAPABILITIES

Because we are self-directing the growth of
our unique gifts and talents toward full potential,
we are able to achieve a solid base of skills, bringing inherent stability into our lives. We see ourselves as possessing more than one gift, one career
path; we seek to bring all of our strengths to maturity. We become flexible and resilient, able to
build our capabilities into unique and exciting
combinations that increase our value to the world.

We are ever more needed by the world in
which we live, and so we are secure. And when
drastic, even threatening changes occur in our surroundings, we have so much to offer that there will
always be new and exciting places for us to apply
our unique gifts and talents. We know we can rely
on our developed capabilities to sustain our success
over an entire lifetime.

Inner STRENGTH

Our identity comes from inside ourselves. It is our rational and realistic understanding of who we are and who we can become. This self-truth begins with awareness of our own humanity — that like all human beings, we possess the ability to be conscious of all that we know. This is the source of intrinsic dignity and self-respect for all human beings. We also come to understand that inner strength resides in our own unique pattern of gifts, talents, and traits.

We are not deluded with fantasies of false capabilities. We better understand how we are the same as or different from others, and we believe in our differences as much as our similarities. The affirmations of others, while heartwarming to receive, no longer form the primary foundations of our identity.

Maximized SUCCESS

We view the self as our primary competitor. Trying to "best" our own "best" is what matters. We take pride in all our efforts, regardless of outcome, and we do not need an opponent in order to produce our highest level of performance. When we engage in competition with others, we seek to succeed fairly and justly, and not at the expense of another's dignity or self-esteem.

Life is no longer a climb to the top. Instead, we understand how we can use our increasing expertise in the process of authentic growth to make life easier as we move along on our journey. Life feels more like taking a pleasant stroll along a gently sloping road, building momentum with passing time. Though the body may fade over time, the spirit is propelled toward the lasting achievement of its true humanity.

Genuine HAPPINESS

No longer confined to a narrow definition equating happiness with fun and recreation, we see that happiness is most genuine when it emanates from the satisfaction of life purpose and the positive effects our lives have on others. Knowing *how* to move toward our future vision, we can bring confidence — yes, happiness — into each day. Sincere happiness is vested in understanding and fulfilling our vision, and in living holistically.

Passion for LIFE

We feel each of our emotions more clearly and deeply, and these emotions allow us to feel more fully alive. We are not passive bystanders to life, feeling little. Nor are we out of control, flooded by feelings that only serve to confuse, overwhelm, and paralyze. In this state of aliveness, we begin to experience the true joy — even ecstasy — that comes from being ourselves and experiencing our true selves in their fullest. These feelings are so irresistible that we instinctively want to access them over and over again.

Unconditional GENEROSITY

Because our understanding of the overall human dilemma increases with our own individual development, we are able to better understand the challenges that others face. We replace feelings of pity and frustration with ones of empathy and compassion. And with this understanding of another's life journey in our minds and hearts, forgiveness flows readily. We are no longer prone to buildups of anger, and we are impervious to acting defensively.

Kindness is a virtue we hold dear. We seek to find the strengths in others instead of focusing on their shortcomings. We purposefully invest time in others with the intention of supporting them in their own quests for a truly human life. We seek remedies and preventions for endemic social problems, recognizing that we possess remarkable powers for affecting others. We share what we have — giving ourselves directly, and transporting our energy through financial resources to areas where we cannot reach directly with our hands.

Authentic LOVE

Amidst a sea of acquaintances, we begin to tire of superficiality and seek quality relationships with greater depth and meaning. We are no longer satisfied by the friendship of only those persons who present a mirror image of our own values and interests. We go beyond loving the reflection of ourselves in others to appreciating individuality and uniqueness. We fall in love with who the other person really is, as opposed to any false fantasy we may foster. We find that together we can create a whole that is much greater than the sum of ourselves.

Growth means that we continually have more to offer one another. We will not tire of each other over time, for we are constantly revealing and sharing all that is new within us. We do not hesitate to enter into this sharing of our innermost feelings and thoughts, because we know that our mutual respect as *truly human* human beings creates a profound level of trust and safety. Our capacity to love expands, so that we experience greater unity with all others and even with the universe itself.

A *Legacy of* IDEAS

We take full advantage of our uniquely human opportunity to share ideas and experiences with others. In so doing, we participate in creating an evolution of thought through the transmission of knowledge and innovation. This mind-to-mind, heart-to-heart, soul-to-soul communication easily outstrips the pace of genetic evolution. Our life's message constitutes a legacy that can continue to influence so many others for years and years, if not centuries and centuries, after our physical death. The very essence of our spirit expresses itself in actions that have a lasting effect on the wisdom available to those that follow us. We are the teachers of the next generation, and we take this responsibility as the greatest privilege of our truly human lives.

These are the benefits that are yours to experience each and every day of your future life.

To what extent are they present in your life today?

To what extent could they be present to you in the future if you embraced change?

This is a decision only you can make for yourself.

THE PATH
OF LEST RISK

*I*f these benefits are so irresistible, so appealing, then why don't we immediately take action? Most often, we hesitate because we believe that change involves risk. Just how often have you allowed the seeming security of the status quo to seduce you into "playing it safe"?

After all, playing it safe *is* a good idea, for the path of least risk is the only realistic way to go about achieving lasting success. Like the concept of the path of least resistance, in which water keeps flowing toward the lowest point in a stream, the path of least risk ensures that energy is conserved so that more can be accomplished in total.

While many others may try to tell you to get over your fears, grit your teeth, and throw yourself headlong into the future, I intend to take a different approach. For I believe that it is in your best interests to follow the course of least risk. As you will see, our current love affair with the status quo is more an issue of not being able to calculate risk than one of realistic fear over what the future may bring.

There are two sides to the risk equation.

In practice, the most frequent error I have observed in risk evaluations is that potential harm is only measured on one side of the equation. When most people or organizations are considering a new action or direction, the first thoughts that come to mind center on all that can possibly go wrong. Sound familiar? Quite possibly so, for the comfort vested in the status quo effectively blinds us to any positive considerations, and causes us to fear change.

A valid risk evaluation analyzes potential outcomes on BOTH sides of the equation. It weighs the cost of moving forward toward your future vision against the cost of staying where you are.

Do you know how to perform a risk evaluation? That's right, there is a specific technique for measuring risk which I want to share with you. In this analysis, we will compare the risk inherent in maintaining the status quo to that of adopting change directed toward attaining your truly human self.

If you are ready, all you need to do is translate the issues I raise to your own specific situation in life.

A thorough understanding of the future benefits of truly human growth is essential.

The real secret to understanding risk is to go beyond fear of failure to *consider what might work out well for you.* This requires an understanding of benefits — the results we achieve when we are successful at living as *truly human* human beings.

By sharing with you in the previous chapter those benefits that I seek to incorporate into my life, I hope you are aware of your opportunity to fill your life to the brim with positive values. This is what your life could be like if you entered into a continuous growth process aimed at achieving your truly human self. Take care not to shy away from the prospect of the good life. Instead, be generous with yourself, for you, by virtue of being human, are worthy of these good outcomes. Unless you color your future vision brightly, you will likely underestimate your fullest possible potential.

We begin our risk analysis with the risk inherent in the status quo. This risk equates to the opportunities we squander when we bypass the range of benefits that could be present to our future selves. To summarize the concept of *missed opportunities* with an equation:

$$\textbf{TOTAL FUTURE BENEFITS} - \textbf{CURRENT BENEFITS} = \textbf{MISSED OPPORTUNITY COST}$$

When calculating current benefits, it is important to remember that more is involved than identifying benefits as either present or absent in daily life. Benefits are not necessarily all-or-nothing phenomena. The extent to which each benefit is currently a part of your life needs to be accounted for. Therefore, benefits might be better assessed as a percentage of what you believe you could achieve in the future.

We can only achieve life's benefits by changing current behaviors.

Now that we have an understanding of the cost of the status quo, measured as *missed opportunity cost,* it is time to evaluate the cost of moving forward with change. The personal growth required to access future benefits does carry a price — a cost to you in changing the substance of your behaviors, your daily way of life. Both the replacement of old habits and the learning of new skills take more energy than simply staying right where you are. This total cost in energy and effort constitutes the risk of moving forward.

This calculation is also one that only you can perform for yourself. It is likely that many different facets of your lifestyle will be affected, and these need your thoughtful consideration.

So this risk analysis comes down to whether you are satisfied with the range and depth of benefits you now receive in life. Or do you desire more? If so, are you willing to put out the necessary energy to learn the skills for your future way of living?

Keep in mind that the extra work is about being engaged in the process of living. So instead of being drudgery, like preparing an income tax return, this process can be an adventure and an exciting investment in knowing and understanding yourself.

60

Which situation represents the lowest cost — that is, the path of least risk? I have no doubt in my mind that the status quo of the present is where the greatest risk in life resides. But there is one final aspect to incorporate in your risk analysis, and that is the damage you incur from persistent frustration.

Compare the frustration associated with learning something new to the loss of *persistent* frustration in your daily life. In practice, the frustration associated with behavioral change is only temporary, because the resulting benefits you seek represent what you really want from life. In contrast, persistent frustration results from doing what you do not want to do. You can only endure these kinds of situations for so long — perhaps as a means to an end, but not as a way of life.

Fear of failure is an illusion.

At this point you may be wondering why I am ignoring the possible failures that may result from deliberate change. This is because fear of failure is only an illusion, and so does not belong in an evaluation of risk.

Think about the effects of living in a continuing state of development, at all times becoming more. In so doing, you will thrive whether a particular venture in life provides results that appear either positive or negative. For on the interior you are always building experience in the business of living — and it is the experience, rather than the specific outcome, that makes you ever more competent at being truly human.

If your capability keeps increasing as you seek to develop yourself, then you become ever more impervious to risk and failure with each step along the way. Perhaps the only real human failure is in not trying to be more. Fortunately, life is not a game of football, in which credit is only given for crossing into the endzone. Effort is what counts. And success flows genuinely from sincere and thoughtful effort.

SECURITY
FACILITATES
STRENGTH

*I*f for any reason you are still holding back from making substantive life change, please allow me to raise a final argument. If the greatest risk is present in the inert state of the status quo, then the rewards of security are yet another most serious reason to embrace a dynamic, changing way of life. Risk is a form of resistance, and it will consume much of your energy and much of your time if you let it. Whenever we allow unnecessary risk to shake our basic sense of security, we short-change our ability to engage in the pursuit of our human potential.

Security is an intrinsic human need.

Just think about it. If your primary concern in life is to find out where your next meal is coming from, that basic need will likely consume your attention until the need is fulfilled. From what state can you best pursue the task of personal development? Isn't a base of security — free from the concerns of survival issues such as food, shelter, and safety — absolutely essential?

I find that business clients too often wait until they are faced with an urgent problem before taking charge of their organization's future. In practice, visioning the future is better accomplished from a position of inherent strength and security, well before a crisis occurs. Whether you are young or old, traditional or alternative, an individualist or a conformist, security is the one need that unites us all. Attaining a secure life is essential to the eventual fulfillment of your purpose as a *truly human* human being.

Knowledge is the basis for security.

So what effect does our assessment of risk as being greatest in the status quo have on our overall security in life? While we may enjoy the comfortable illusion of security in our present way of living and doing, feeling comfortable with the familiar is quite different from achieving all that you are meant to achieve. If you choose to stay with what's right in front of you, you may be forestalling your chance to access your ultimate self.

The saying "ignorance is bliss" can never be true if your goal is success over the course of a lifetime. Only knowledge, translated into a vision of your future self, can allow you to move beyond today's tried and true to find your unique truth.

I know for a fact that I have a long way to go in the pursuit of my complete self. And I know that

today I am less than what I can become in the future.
After all, who among us has exhausted all possibilities for further development during the time in
which we inhabit our physical bodies? If you're at
all like me, then you know you also have a long way
to go; it's just that sometimes we are afraid that
future change will set us back instead of ahead.

**Security increases as you progress
toward your truly human self.**

Think more deeply about the concept of security and ask yourself, "When will I be most secure?"
Does security in life increase when we pursue our
complete selves? I believe so. For ultimate security
is one that *you* control, rather than a state that
depends on the thoughtful generosity of others.

Security, for me, is virtually synonymous
with being self-sufficient, a self-made person. For
when I am dependent, I am avoiding my own
humanity. And because this avoidance can short-
change the development of my capabilities, when
life circumstances change, I may not be ready to
meet a new challenge successfully.

COMING
FULL
CIRCLE

*A*s I allow myself to explore all the benefits of truly human growth, I realize that these benefits are not reserved for some future endpoint or ultimate reward for a job well done. There is no fixed endpoint to my vision of a *truly human* human being. Rather, these benefits accrue as progress is made in the process of growth. The possibilities that my unique nature and nurture create for my future are irresistible. They constitute a state of continuing opportunities, and as I participate in a seamless and self-directed process for growth, these benefits will continue to reveal themselves ever more fully to me.

By looking for the presence of these benefits as I progress further in my growth, I am affirming that my growth is authentic. And no matter how far I progress on this truly human journey, I know that the future holds more for me than the present. Risk and insecurity remain greatest in the status quo. Growth is my best protection in an ever-changing world. As I reach for my vision, I find that it keeps transforming, presenting me with a future that is even richer, more fulfilling, than today. The vision itself is in a state of constant evolution, always providing the challenge and motivation for excellence.

66   Now we have brought our evaluation of risk full circle. Which side of the risk equation presents the path of least risk in your life? Is it worth maintaining the status quo now that you are better prepared to understand the cost of missed opportunities? Or will you discover that by embracing life-changing growth toward your truly human self, you can access lasting security and authentic success?

What's next?

If growth is to become our ongoing state of life, then we need to learn *how* to grow *strategically*. In this way, the growth we undertake will maximize the likelihood of achieving authentic success.

PART FIVE

PROVEN

SUCCESS

HOW
TO
GROW

When I stop to think about it, I realize that no one has ever summarized for me the process of growth. Can you recall a day in school when growth was explained in terms you could easily apply to your own life? Did your parents ever teach you the facts of growth?

There's no doubt that the process of being alive is most complex. While in various college biology and bacteriology courses, I ran experiments demonstrating how optimal growth occurs when plenty of nutrients and minimal amounts of toxins are present in the surrounding environment. I researched how bacteria were affected by the presence of penicillin, and found out how persistent these organisms could be in the business of staying alive when the fluid surrounding them was similar to the salty muck inside their cells.

But throughout all of my biological studies, we were quite cavalier about the application of the word *growth*. In fact, we casually talked about growth when what we actually studied were rates

of cell division. I guess it was difficult to see the big picture in life when we were so focused on the sea of bacteria in our test tubes.

The building blocks of life itself are designed for replication.

Like the bacteria I studied, the very building blocks of life itself are also concerned with the task of replication. The architecture of DNA, deoxyribonucleic acid, is a double-helical structure, consisting of two interwoven and complementary strands. It has been a focus of scientific inquiry ever since its discovery by James Watson, Francis Crick, and Rosalind Franklin. But whether making DNA, or transmitting instructions as RNA (ribonucleic acid) to make proteins that initiate, maintain, or stop functions at the cellular level, DNA is concerned about making an *exact duplicate* — a replica of all or part of itself.

Human reproduction, like replication, also needs to be clearly differentiated from growth. For reproduction results in the merging of two unique and separate genomes to create one or more new individual members of our species.

In order to prepare for reproduction, humans pass through a physical transformation from juvenile to adult. This transformation is preprogrammed within us, just as it is for all mammals. Because it occurs without conscious decision making, and involves a flamboyant transformation in the very form of the organism, in my mind, puberty is closer to the process of metamorphosis than the process of human growth I seek to describe. In a sense, because this change is so visible and so genetically driven, physical maturation in humans is not unlike the transformation of tadpole to frog, or caterpillar to butterfly.

Beyond this physical change, we humans are pretty much left to engage in growth that is centered on our inner lives. Physical growth in adults becomes, for all practical purposes, limited to prevention, training, maintenance, and repair. The shift from body to soul and the capacity to figure things out on our own predominate for the rest of our lives, thanks to heightened consciousness.

Are we capable of this growth?

While philosophers, psychologists, and neurobiologists will continue to explore what constitutes human growth and the nature of our heightened consciousness, we cannot wait for their ultimate conclusions. Rather, we need to proceed in our own process of personal growth, confident in our innate ability to undertake this challenge.

If we are human, then we know that each of us carries the secrets to achieving the development of

our humanity. Each of us has already been well prepared, equipped by genetic heritage, to undertake
human growth. But we may need considerable practice to mature our abilities.

So how could I best translate the process of
growth to a personal level? The inner growth I wanted to understand is intangible. It means making
more of my spirit — which cannot be pinpointed
inside the molecules that comprise my physical being.
The task seemed overwhelming at first, given the
sheer complexity of the human body and spirit.

**A *physical model* can be most helpful
in defining that which is intangible.**

What I needed was something tangible to
represent this invisible essence of the spirit. If there
was something I could see — or better yet, touch,
hold and feel — then it might be easier to get going.

I had ideas of where to look, because my
study of science had shown me that nature likes to
repeat any design proven successful; for example,
the residual pattern of molecules in a gas is not
unlike the swirl of the cosmos itself. If nature draws
physical parallels between structures of vastly different sizes and magnitudes of energy, why couldn't I
find a parallel between the physical world and the
seemingly invisible content of my self — my inner
energy and life force?

Nature provides clues which can foster our understanding of growth.

72 In that sense, my approach was simplified. I would look for success that already exists in nature. There was no need to reinvent what was already waiting to be discovered; I would simply use what nature has already shown to favor in its ongoing process of selection. Less energy wasted all around. Now all I had to do was find a visible example of growth. This is the process of identifying a model, whose behavior I can study on a smaller, simpler scale and then extrapolate to my own.

So should I choose the organism I felt closest to, my cat Truffles? Well, not exactly; she's also too complex to qualify as a good model. Something even simpler was needed, but it still had to follow the overall definition I had established for growth — that is, *growth makes more of the same without changing the essential form.* A tree fits this description, but somehow the idea of using a tree didn't resonate with me personally. Maybe I needed more selection criteria to help me make a better choice.

Defining selection criteria facilitates the choice of an effective model.

When I gave human growth more thought, I realized that I wanted my model to affirm my individuality. Accordingly, I wanted to study growth in

a form of life that supports diversity. It also followed that I wanted the organism to have been successful over a very long period of time, for if my model had survived this long, it had already figured out how to do more with less energy.

Millions of years would be good, hundreds of millions of years even better. Why not use something that's been around even longer than humankind? I might learn something nature already knows that we humans forget to consider, since as a species, we are still just newcomers to life on this planet earth.

And so I kept on looking, and waiting patiently for that moment of insight — the discovery of my model — to occur.

A MOMENT
OF AWARENESS

By their very nature, moments of insight happen quite unexpectedly. For me, such a day occurred during a recent visit to St. Thomas in 1997. On that particular day, I decided to take a leisurely stroll around the town of Charlotte Amalie.

I made my way along Main Street, where crowds of passengers from the many ships in port had only a few hours to search for the brilliant gold and diamonds, fine watches, and trendy fashions that beckoned from store windows. Seeking refuge from the swarm of shoppers, I turned onto an inconspicuous, narrow cobblestone alley. There, near the alley's end, was a quaint shop that unassumingly brought together treasures from all around the world: an eclectic assortment of antiques and artifacts recalling other times and places.

There I saw, scattered between the handmade ceramics and figurines, nature's own reminders of how growth occurred long before we humans walked on this earth. First, my eye was caught by a fossilized ammonite that glistened with golden-colored iron pyrite deposits. This mineralized shell dated back to the Jurassic period, providing a most simple example of growth — a coil, not unlike a garden hose that wraps around itself. But in this case, the size of the coil *grew steadily larger* with increasing length.

Pyrite ammonite fossil.
Location: Germany. Date: Jurassic Period, approximately 180 million years old.

Making more without changing its basic form, this ammonite fossil not only illustrated growth, but brought my definition of growth to life. I was grateful to the soft-bodied creature that constructed this shell for leaving behind a powerful message I would eventually stumble upon some 180 million years later.

76   I continued my exploration of the store, only to encounter another shell fossil which was also based on an expanding coil. But unlike the ammonite, whose coil wound on a single plane, this second fossil, a casting of a turritella, moved through three-dimensional space as it grew. Beginning at one very tiny end, the coil grew both outward and forward with increasing length, forming a cone. This coil ventured successfully into a new dimension, all the while staying true to its essential form.

Both fossils were indeed dramatic examples of the definition of growth, but with significant differences. The ammonite's coil was walled off into many separate chambers and bound to growth on a plane; the other demonstrated a continuous, seamless flow of growth in all three dimensions. I immediately felt greater affinity for the latter fossil.

This photographic illustration shows how the turritella fossil grew with each turn in its coil. Location: Java, Indonesia. Date: Pliocene Period, approximately 5 million years old.

I left St. Thomas with these fossils, knowing that there was still much more to be learned from them. My first destination upon returning home was San Francisco's Steinhart Aquarium, where in the bookstore, I came across Leonard Hill's *Shells — Treasures of the Sea.* Combing the pages, I soon learned that the ammonite went into extinction about 65 million years ago. The shell that most closely resembles the ammonite's architectural form today is the nautilus, which is part of a handful of species belonging to *Cephalopoda* — a class predominated by numerous varieties of octopi.

In contrast, the turritella fossil was a member of class *Gastropoda,* which presents an enormous range of diversity. There are more than 80,000 known species, noteworthy for their tremendous ability to adapt to changing environments. After reading through several sources of information, I learned that these gastropods continue to flourish today as they have for hundreds of millions of years, with different species able to withstand the heat of boiling water or the chill of frozen ice; to evolve from the salinity of ocean water to thrive in fresh water streams; and to move from dwelling at ocean's bottom onto shorelines, then onto land and eventually up into trees.

Gastropods, without hesitation, became my personal choice, meeting all the test criteria I had established for a model of authentic growth. And they were especially endearing for their ability to explore multiple dimensions, just as I myself seek to explore the dimensions of my own mind and soul.

78   Noticing that the magnificent photos of shells in this coffee-table-sized volume had been taken by nature photographer Pete Carmichael, I was quickly on the phone to Florida, chatting with him. I told him of my desire to study gastropod forms as a means for better understanding my own growth. Within a few days, over 500 slides of different gastropod species arrived from Pete, ready for me to absorb.

Looking at one slide after the other, over and over again, I filled my head with the wondrous diversity of the gastropods, all the while marveling at how similar their architecture was. Somehow, a common structure had facilitated a seemingly unlimited freedom to respond to their surrounding and ever-evolving world. Stripes and intricate spotted patterns characterized some, while others boasted ribs, wings, and spines. Some were flat, some were elongated so that they could anchor their shells in the mud. All so different, yet all so much the same.

While on these journeys, I imagined taking these creatures into my hands, feeling their different textures, examining variations in color and patterns, wondering where they lived, and then holding each

to my ear, listening for the haunting sounds of the ocean inside.

You too may wish to take this journey. The following pages present a few of the shell photographs that became most prominent in my consideration of my own growth process. If you choose to join me, take time to consider each of the shells as individual forms. Then stand back and consider how the shells are similar to or different from each other.

Take care not to censor your thoughts. Allow ideas or associations to unfold and lead you to others. But always remember to let these shells engage each of your senses. Enjoy, as I have, what nature brings you, for in a state of enjoyment you are most likely to discover insights into your own future vision — and the process for growth toward this vision.

What's next?

Following this photo essay, I will share with you the conclusions I have reached and that I use to guide my own inner growth.

Shell Essay

Photos by Pete Carmichael

Astraea phoebia, LONG-SPINED STAR SHELL

Trochus virgatus, STRIPED TOP SHELL

Chicoreus cichoreum, ENDIVE MUREX

Thatcheria mirabilis, JAPANESE WONDER SHELL

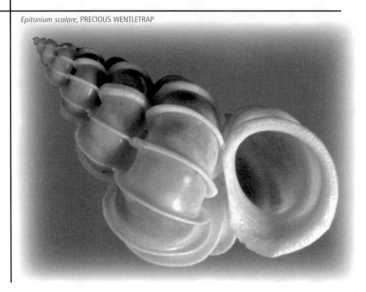

Epitonium scalare, PRECIOUS WENTLETRAP

Looking down on the helical coil of Thatcheria mirabilis, JAPANESE WONDER SHELL

Charonia tritonis, PACIFIC TRITON'S TRUMPET

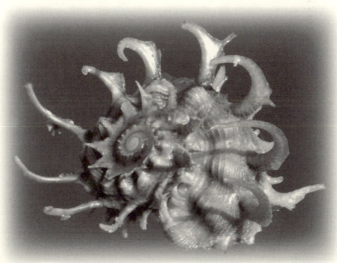

Angaria sphaerula, KIENER'S DELPHINULA

Neptunea tabulata, TABLED NEPTUNE

86

Busycon canaliculatum, CHANNELED WHELK

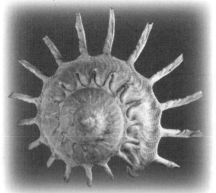

Stellaria solaris, SUNBURST CARRIER SHELL

87

Latiaxis vicdani, VICTOR DAN'S LATIAXIS and *Hirtomurex teremachii*, TEREMACHI'S LATIAXIS

Astraea phoebia, LONG-SPINED STAR SHELL

Architectonica perspectiva, CLEAR SUNDIAL

Visit www.umano.com
*to view these photographs in full color
and read about their histories.*

Trigonostoma milleri, MILLER'S NUTMEG

PART SIX

PRINCIPLES

OF

GROWTH

THE
JOURNEY
CONTINUES

I continued to take my visual journeys with the images of gastropod shells. More often than not, the results were less than what I hoped for. I had to be patient, to learn to live with the chaos of all these many images inside my mind. At times it was definitely frustrating. But because I had taken these types of journeys before, I had a basic trust in my ability to eventually reach conclusions.

My goal was to draw out of my thinking a series of principles that I could use to guide my growth. The principles would need to be universal in nature; that is, they would be applicable to any phase or aspect of my life. They would serve as a framework, not unlike that which the shell provides to the delicate organism it contains.

If the *strategies* (how to attain a specific goal) I developed incorporated these principles, I would be able to reach decisions that were unique to each situation, but also consistent in upholding the vision that I saw for myself as a *truly human* human being. By selecting the growth strategy that best

reflected the principles, I would be able to increase my plan's likelihood of success.

Was I motivated? Yes; the results would allow me to undertake my own growth with greater confidence, because I was developing guidelines to help me determine if my process was authentic.

91

As my reflection proceeded, different thoughts emerged. At first, my mind was filled with observations about shell architecture. From the smallest of beginnings, the shell's coil grows, making more of the same without changing its essential form. By pushing both forward and outward, the shell becomes proportionally larger.

Origin/Nucleus
The point where shell growth begins.

Coil
The shell is formed by a coil which enlarges with increasing length.

Varices
Denote periods of rest between phases of growth.

Orifice/Aperture
Opening through which the organism encounters the world.

Epitonium scalare, PRECIOUS WENTLETRAP

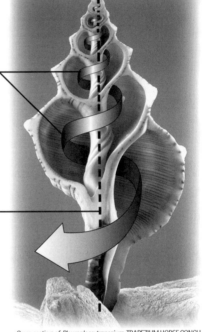

The shell defines the space in which the organism lives, as well as a central axis or core.

92

Chamber (ARROW)
The space which the organism occupies is continuous and without walls.

Axis
The core created by the shell's coil is asymmetrical.

Cross-section of *Pleuroploca trapezium*, TRAPEZIUM HORSE CONCH

In particular, I noticed how gastropod shells share a single structure, known as the *logarithmic spiral*. Simply put, there is a single mathematical truth behind the construction of each gastropod species' shell. The size of the shell's growing edge — its circumference — can be calculated using the same factor (a number used to multiply the increasing length of the coil). This proportional relationship provides the shell with stability, even amidst the ebb and flow of ocean waves.

Looking down on a shell, each turn in the shell's coil, called a whorl, appears essentially the same — just proportionately larger. Growth is steady and always in keeping with the definition of making more without altering the form.

93

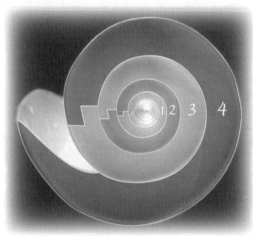

Whorl
One complete 360° revolution of the shell's coil.

1,2,3,4
Shaded areas illustrate 4 separate whorls.

Thatcheria mirabilis, JAPANESE WONDER SHELL

Yet at the same time, I see how different each species of gastropod is from the others. Somehow, the presence of this consistent mathematical truth does not restrict the ability of the organism to reshape the expression of this truth through a process of natural selection.

Order lives hand-in-hand with experimentation and diversity.

The more I thought and read about this basic design in nature, the more I realized how enchanted humans have been throughout history with this form of the outward logarithmic spiral. In ancient times, it was the basis for the Greek key design and the proportions between the height and width of the Parthenon, as well as the guiding architectural principle behind European Gothic cathedrals and the pyramids of Egypt. Leonardo da Vinci showed us how this proportion is reflected in the design of the human body, and perhaps for this reason we are innately attracted to the order embodied in the outward spiral. We see it as beautiful, and in turn, we see the beauty in each of us.

And when I came to think about it, the shell was a prominent form that I had always sought to incorporate into my life. Whether as actual shells left behind by their former inhabitants, or as images in art, they were always there, always a source of continuing attraction and inspiration.

The more I reflected on the implications of the outward spiral for my own growth, the more I also became aware of how prevalent its form is in the world that currently surrounds me.

It is a popular symbol in corporate logos, whether in Sybase's depiction of the Golden Mean (a logarithmic spiral depicted on a single plane), or MindSpring's profile of a human head that emanates from an outward spiral. The Japanese Wonder Shell was also Frank Lloyd Wright's inspiration for the architecture of the Guggenheim Museum in New

York City. I will never forget this grand, larger-than-life embodiment of something so simple as a shell. No matter where I look, where I go, I see the outward spiral's message of growth and vitality.

These thoughts about shell architecture evolved into insights about how the shell could serve as a metaphor for my own life, and in turn form the basis for growth principles. By drawing parallels between shell architecture and my own process for growth, I could find growth strategies that had already been proven and encoded into nature's design. My task would be to simplify the complexity of shells by distilling out shared features of their growth.

To do this I welcomed all ideas that emerged, whether seemingly trivial or profound. Then, and only then, did I begin a systematic process for qualifying the ideas against my established criteria for human growth. Only at the very end of idea generation did I translate the visual images into words on the pages that follow.

Here are my results. As always, take from this discussion anything that you believe will bring value to your own process for growth. And do not hesitate to formulate your own principles. Just take care to assure that your conclusions uphold your personal vision as a *truly human* human being, and cause you to be *strategic* in how you go about growing.

The Principle of
DIMENSIONS

*Growth expands to fill multidimensional space,
thereby creating ideas.*

The gastropods developed an innovative way to make more room for the delicate, soft-bodied creatures they contain. Each shell expands the space available for the organism's growth by extending its architecture not just forward but outward as well.

Revolution upon revolution, always reaching further, wider, higher, deeper, so that from a very small beginning, a larger and larger volume of space is encompassed within its structure.

If I am to be successful at achieving authentic growth, then I cannot be limited to thinking on a single plane to join two points. Instead, I must create space for ideas by bursting through to the multiple dimensions of my inner self.

For there in that space and volume, amidst a profusion of previously unrelated bits and bytes of information, I thrive on bringing order to chaos. I can encourage my mind to look in all directions in order to enter the realm of the abstract, the conceptual. I become an adventurer, pioneer-

ing and probing through inner space. Like the gastropod's shell, I am always reaching further, wider, higher, deeper. Here I find I can make linkages and metaphors between seemingly unrelated concepts. My thoughts grow into truly human ideas — ideas which are proof of the creative power inherent to each and every human being.

As my spirit grows in multiple dimensions, I find that I want to partake ever more fully in my world, interacting with all that surrounds me. More of the universe comes within my grasp and feeds and inspires my soul. And so, from a very small beginning, I grow to fill myself with the stuff of dreams. Then I create my authentic self, propelled toward the future vision my conceptual mind creates for me.

The *Principle* of
PHYSICALITY

Growth utilizes the physical body so that the spirit ever more fully encounters the surrounding world.

The shell's architecture is much like a scaffold, protecting the organism inside without restricting its growth. The shell defines shape for an otherwise shapeless organism. The space defined by the scaffold is not so tight that the organism cannot continue to expand. There is room to become more.

This scaffold can also be depended upon for continuing support. The gastropod can draw within this protective house to rest and renew itself, or it can probe outside, using fluid and dynamic movements to explore its world. The organism always demonstrates great respect for the value its shell provides, and devotes enormous and immediate energy to repairing any damage to the shell's integrity as a holistic structure.

I can similarly view my body as a scaffold, for it contains and supports my thoughts and my spirit, but never restricts them from moving through space. Because I exist in a real, physical world, and not simply in a realm of ideas, information comes to me through my body. Just as gastropods define an aperture to interface with the surrounding world, we humans similarly depend upon our physical bodies as vehicles for communication and interaction with our world. By reaching out, we find the sensory information — the sights, sounds, smells, textures, and tastes comprising our environment — that feeds our hearts and minds.

My growth, then, is in part contingent upon becoming thoroughly immersed in the world, acting and interacting as part of a human community and a universal community of all living things. But at times, growth also requires a retreat from the world into the protected environment of my inner life. Here I rest, renew, and create myself in preparation for my next encounter with all that surrounds me. My body is the house of my soul. Its structure helps me to impact my world with lasting effect.

I am reminded to pay attention to the health and well-being of my physical self, knowing its essential role in my growth. After all, mind, body, and spirit work best as an integral whole.

The Principle of
VALUES

100

*Growth is shaped by a dynamic core of values
that upholds what is truly human.*

An empty space acts as an invisible axis
around which the growing coil of the gastropod shell
wraps itself. But this axis is not a straight line; it
winds asymmetrically inside the shell's coil, always
in sync with the forward movement of growth.

I like to think of this
core as a metaphor for my
values and beliefs, which
seem thin as air, yet shape
and define my entire being.
Here, at the very core of my
being, I form a system of
life-defining values to continually evolve and shape
my spirit. These values,
which I think through and
use to make life choices,

define the actions and decisions I will use to propel
myself toward my truly human life purpose.

Just as the shell's central axis continues to extend itself at the growing edge of the coil, so too, my values continue to develop as I grow. Experience deepens my conviction in what I believe, and in my ability to use these values wisely as guidelines for sound morals and ethical decision making.

But reinterpreting core values in response to the changing circumstances that life poses for me is a never-ending challenge. Each new decision must be relevant to the real world, just as those made in the past were relevant to the unique times and circumstances of the past.

Here, in the intimate interface between my actions and my core values, I learn who I am and what I stand for. I recognize that these values represent my most basic decisions about how I will live my life. For example, if I have made the decision to achieve my full potential, what values will guide the implementation of my decision? Will I place self-interest as my overriding intention, or I will I choose to value other individuals, respecting their quests for authentic growth as well as my own? Will I simply define my pursuit as one that does not harm others? Or will I choose the most truly human option, and commit to a life that directly benefits others as well as myself?

The Principle of
PROPORTIONALITY

Growth maintains a proportional relationship between the past, the present, and the future, to secure lasting strength and stability.

Each gastropod shell is a coil whose growing edge becomes increasingly larger as it extends in length. Growth is steady and continuous, always providing more without risking overall stability.

This is the benefit that the mathematical truth contained in gastropod architecture brings to its organism. This secret to the shell's success is a proportional relationship, which links what has come before to what is happening in the present, and to what can happen in the future.

Whether the shell's structure is composed of just a few larger revolutions in its spiral or many tightly wound ones, proportionality is at work. By maintaining physical contact between each revolution in the spiral, the shell maximizes the strength of

its structure. Those shells that are wound loosely, each revolution dangling into space, risk instability.

Proportionality can be generalized, as a metaphor for human growth, to mean harmony and balance between cycles of self-directed growth over the course of an entire lifetime.

103

To incorporate proportionality into our lives, we remain aware that as we move forward, we also stay connected to the past. This means more than simply remembering what has come before. It means bringing the best outcomes of prior growth into our *new* growth. Growth commingles old with new so that there is always a stable base of experience from which to expand.

My task is to continually challenge myself with some proportion of newness. I reach out more widely for what was previously out of reach, stretching myself into the future but never reaching so far that I disconnect from what has already been achieved. Never too much, never too little, always just the right and consistent amount of expansion as growth proceeds.

Through the strength conferred by proportionality, we will be prepared to thrive within the fluctuating rhythm of life's challenges. We, too, can stand strong in the midst of the waves.

The Principle of
MASTERY

Growth, with experience, allows more to be accomplished with less effort.

Looking down on the outward spiral of the gastropod shell, I can envision my growth as a series of 360-degree phases — each revolution or complete turn of the spiral signifying a new phase of growth, each always more expansive than the previous one, but otherwise appearing similar to all others.

Growth can be thought of as a process that regularly repeats itself. And in that planned repetition, with time and experience, the organism must somehow learn to do more with the same or with even less effort, thereby conserving valuable energy.

Because of this construction, there is a wisdom that builds from one phase of growth to the

next. It appears as though the shell practices growing over and over again, and in so doing *trains itself* in how to grow.

I can envision each major phase of my own growth as a turn in the shell's spiral. And if I make sure each phase of self-directed growth encompasses the same sequence and scope of activities, I can continually make better use of my energy. When the phases of growth are consistent from one to the next, I can ultimately master the process of growth.

In my vision of growth, each phase begins with the development of a *strategic plan*. The first stage of plan implementation is *learning*, which leads to the mastery of skills. These new generic skills are *individualized* to bring forth my own unique gifts and talents. Next, this original outcome is expressed and shared with others as *creative actions*. Finally, a time of *rest and renewal* follows, during which I absorb the reactions of others and assess change in the world to guide the next phase of my growth.

Each new phase of growth repeats this very same sequence of activities. I soon become an expert in planning, learning, individualizing, sharing, and renewing. As I build greater mastery in the process of growth, I can increasingly focus more effort on the *quality* and *uniqueness* of growth outcomes, and less on the process of growth itself.

The Principle of
ADAPTABILITY

*Growth deliberately adapts the self in anticipation
of change.*

Experimentation is programmed into the fabric of the gastropod, producing over time an endless variety of shell shapes. Each gastropod species has searched and found the adaptation that allows it to thrive in the midst of an ever-changing world. Through a process of random trial and error, success has been discovered.

I, too, must be flexible and adaptable, but I have a powerful advantage over gastropods. I can

use my firsthand knowledge to forecast coming change, and then *deliberately* choose those adaptations in my life strategy that will allow me to preserve and extend success. I am not

limited to random trials, but can use wisdom to make educated predictions of my best course of action.

This is the essence of strategic planning, which brings my long-term vision as a truly human human being into reality. Here I differ vastly from the gastropod. In human life, adaptability becomes one of the primary expressions of my ability to be aware of all that I know.

Heightened consciousness allows me to direct my own evolutionary process in miniature, learning through educated guesstimates how to better predict external change in the world. As I implement different adaptations, I evaluate what works well in my relationship with the world surrounding me, and can then choose to incorporate into my way of life only those experiments that are successful. Adaptability to changing circumstances, or even to threats in my environment, assures not only my survival, but facilitates continuing inner growth.

Vigilant observation is prerequisite to predicting change in our surroundings. We become attentive to clues that foretell change. As a result, we can forecast how we might translate our ideas and actions to remain relevant within a system of dynamic change. And so, we are able to respond and react in ways that replace random trial and error with intelligent planning.

The Principle of
EXCELLENCE

Growth seeks excellence over perfection, and in so doing mitigates fear.

The gastropod has accepted asymmetry in order to push into the third dimension and access more space for the organism it supports. This is in contrast to the nautilus shell, which approaches absolute beauty and perfection because of its symmetry. But in making this aesthetic sacrifice, gastropods have generated thousands upon thousands of successful species. In a sense, the nautilus' perfect beauty

pales in comparison, because its symmetrical structure is limiting and eventually precludes the experimentation that is necessary for diversity.

For me, as for the gastropod, excellence is the most realistic and valid goal, as perfection asks for a flawlessness that is essentially unobtainable. If I view perfection as my goal and fall short, I can only regard myself as losing, failing, even being inherently

flawed. Excellence centers on the importance of the process and not just the final result. It is accepting of the small imperfections that result from trying new and different approaches. Excellence is steady and forgiving; pursuing excellence motivates me to keep on S-T-R-E-T-C-H-I-N-G for my goals.

Most of us inspire our actions with good intentions. While our educated guesses will prove to work better at some times than at others, intention is key. The terms "failure" and "flawed" should be reserved for those who deliberately choose to act from positions of ignorance and arrogance — not for those who make an honest effort in accordance with their truly human vision.

If we set proper expectations for our outcomes, fear of failure can become a non-issue. When we see each decision — each step we take toward our vision of excellence — as an information-gathering expedition, then there is no such thing as failure. Actions are like scientific experiments, and if we have our consciousness tuned in to interpret all that happens, any action we take will yield something to be learned. There is nothing to fear when information, rather than a specific result, is our goal.

VIII
The Principle of
MYSTERY

Growth is continually motivated by the mystery of life.

Much of human growth can be summarized as the search for truth. As humans, we are inherently predisposed to seeking out the underlying order in things, interpreting all of creation as a means of better understanding ourselves.

Much has been learned, yet there is still so much to be discovered. And so today's scientists and philosophers continue to pursue the truth vigorously.

I believe this truth is the most fundamental principle of growth. While we know much about our inner growth, it is still in greatest part a mystery. Though we seek to devise metaphors and principles that will keep us true to our definition of authentic human growth, we move through the void that time creates knowing it still remains essentially unknown.

That we as humans are blessed with the powers of heightened consciousness, creativity, and individuality is our essential truth, and in that truth lies our essential *dignity*. That we are still such infants

in the process of understanding the total truth of creation is our essential *humility*.

And so, growth involves surrender to all that remains unknown. While we can make educated guesstimates about the future, we cannot predict what will actually happen. But there is no need to recoil from the unknown, for we have already discovered how to secure and strengthen our growth through the incorporation of these principles into our strategies for the future.

There is always an element of mystery, of unanticipated challenge, that demands flexibility. And it is from a position of active growth, rather than the motionless status quo, that we are better prepared for life's mysteries. Indeed, the process of becoming more makes us capable of change.

In this way, mystery is unquestionably necessary, for our inexhaustible curiosity regarding the unknown — the desire to solve the mystery — keeps us motivated to pursue future growth. It is the nature of human beings to always want answers to the questions "Why?" "What if?" and "How does this work?" We are indeed hunters of information and gatherers of knowledge. We exist to push limits. In the end, mystery is a most potent seductress for human beings. It inspires peak human performance, for as we seek to understand the unknown, we create our truly human selves.

The Principles of
Truly Human
GROWTH

The Principle of
DIMENSIONS

Growth expands to fill multidimensional space, thereby creating ideas.

The Principle of
PHYSICALITY

Growth utilizes the physical body so that the spirit ever more fully encounters the surrounding world.

The Principle of
VALUES

Growth is shaped by a dynamic core of values that upholds what is truly human.

The Principle of
PROPORTIONALITY

Growth maintains a proportional relationship between the past, the present, and the future, to secure lasting strength and stability.

The Principle of
MASTERY

*Growth, with experience,
allows more to be
accomplished with less effort.*

The Principle of
ADAPTABILITY

*Growth deliberately adapts
the self in anticipation of
change.*

The Principle of
EXCELLENCE

*Growth seeks excellence
over perfection, and in so
doing mitigates fear.*

The Principle of
MYSTERY

*Growth is continually
motivated by the mystery
of life.*

GUIDELINES, NOT RULES

The **Principles of Truly Human Growth** can help you become strategic in how you go about growth, thereby increasing the likelihood of success. For to the extent that these principles of growth are embodied in your plans and actions, risk will diminish, while security heightens. Each of us will move closer to our individual visions.

To achieve the greatest benefit from these principles, think of them as guidelines and avoid translating them into hard and fast rules. To help you, I have kept my descriptions of the principles to a minimum. The further I define the principles and how they might be interpreted in specific life situations, the more likely they will be translated into laws — lists of do's and don'ts. In this rigidly delineated form, I would give you nothing more than an excuse to revert to the status quo.

Think about it: when the process for growth becomes strictly governed by rules, inner growth is much less likely to occur. This is because the rules of growth will be driving you instead of *you* making

the decisions that keep your growth process authentic. Quality thinking is suspended, in preference for rote memorization and application of the rules. What could have been a life's journey is now reduced to a game. As I have said before, life on autopilot is not a human option.

When a rule-driven, prescribed way to grow is introduced into a time-cramming way of life, we only manage to further numb ourselves to the reality of life and to increase our dissatisfaction at day's end. Heightened consciousness — being aware of all that you know — is the prerequisite for authenticity. We always grow our own inner selves. It is not something I can do for you, nor you for me. Each of us is called to use the highest capacities of our minds to internalize the growth principles, and then to continually rework their meaning in light of changing circumstances.

And so, we will achieve greater success if we engage these principles as guidelines for qualifying the relevance and validity of each new plan. This requires an active mind, one which goes beyond thinking along a line or choosing between forks in the path ahead. Our ability to apply the *First Principle of Growth* — to think through and visualize our future selves in multiple dimensions — will likely become a make-or-break issue for many among us.

Through years of observation, this is what my client experience has shown me to be the most formidable barrier to individual and organizational growth.

116   It is my belief that this inability to vision in multiple dimensions is the most significant threat to human growth created by our productivity- and time-obsessed society. But this need not be the outcome. Instead of being confined by productivity, let us all learn to use its techniques constructively to free our thinking for matters of heightened consciousness — just as the shared, mathematically defined architecture of gastropod shells liberates the organisms to encounter the world. Let us create a climate for the kind of thinking that will allow us to bring the *Principles of Truly Human Growth* to life with each and every new decision we make.

What's next?

How to remove possible barriers to the *Principle of Multiple Dimensions*, by learning the differences between linear and conceptual approaches so that you can enter more effectively into the realm of holistic thinking.

PART SEVEN

HOLISTIC

THINKING

THINKING
ABOUT
THINKING

Do you ever think about how you think? Have you ever noticed how you use your mind in different situations, such as organizing your day or generating ideas? Do you deliberately evaluate the outcomes of decisions to find ways to improve how you think?

Understanding thinking poses one of the greatest challenges to our awareness of what we know. But by turning our thinking capabilities in on themselves, we can watch ourselves think. And we can use this heightened awareness to develop the specialized thinking skills requisite for strategic vision.

This is essential, because effective visioning requires the kind of conceptual thinking that allows you to see the big picture — all the days of your life viewed in the context of an entire lifetime. For it is from this perspective that you can mold fragments into a new and meaningful whole. If that sounds like a mysterious task, it is only because we too often live our lives within a productivity-based, regimented daily structure. We too often find ourselves focused

on details, the passage of time, and problem-solving; in other words, we habitually think along a line rather than in multidimensional space, where ideas are formed. Successful strategic visioning depends on the integrated use of both the conceptual and the linear. The transition between the two modes of thinking is the most frequent stumbling block to visioning that I have observed among my clients.

All that is needed is practice.

I want you to master the ability to transition between linear and conceptual thinking modes for yourself as well. All that is needed is a good understanding of the hallmarks of these two types of thinking, linear and conceptual; when each type is best used; and how to gain the necessary practice in using them to your best advantage.

A WORLD OF DIFFERENCE

Conceptual, abstract, spatial thinking forms the basis of our ability to create something new from all the pieces of information in us and around us. This thinking includes the creative process, as well as the ability to see the big picture.

By thinking spatially in multiple dimensions, we can probe life's countless relationships. We draw metaphors, like the one between shell architecture and human growth. We make linkages between seemingly unrelated thoughts, and our favorite question is "what if?" If you have ever tried to "read" the meaning behind actions, or the emotional reactions of others, then you are already using conceptual thinking and may be well on your way to becoming adept at visioning.

Conceptual thinking is bright and vibrant, soft and curving. Its scope is large and visionary and filled with newness. It includes flights of fantasy and fiction. This kind of thinking can take you places you will never physically visit because they exist only in the inner recesses of your mind.

Conceptual thinking can feel more difficult and rigorous than linear thinking because we tend to use it less often — and because it asks you to put everything you know into simultaneous consideration. Thus, by allowing your mind's eye to see in all directions, you will have the best possible vantage point from which to generate ideas.

The wisdom of past experience casts beacons of light into the boundless space that surrounds you. Your vision improves, but is not completely clear, for the past cannot completely forecast the future. This is where your humanity comes into its fullest expression. You, and only you, can create a vision of yourself at your absolute best.

Information about who you are, where you come from, and the people and circumstances that surround you, can now be integrated and shaped into scenarios. These possible futures will reveal themselves to you as alternative ways of living your days.

Surrender is necessary. You are an observer watching your own mind at work, trusting that you will achieve your visionary goal. Just sit back and release your mind.

Everything and every option is now in view, all at the same time. You're a juggler, with all the balls of possibility cycling in the foggy air of your conscious and unconscious minds. The tension builds as you grasp through the partial darkness to catch each ball and place it into motion once again. Then suddenly, when you least expect it, the fog clears. A new synthesis of information emerges in the form of an idea, a vision of what can be, ready for your thoughtful consideration.

122

Chaos, which is multidimensional, is the state from which most innovations and creative ideas emerge. While this is a more frustrating environment from which to think in the short term, the consideration of all possible dimensions inherently lowers risk in the long term. It forces us to be fully engaged as human beings: intellectually, emotionally, and physically, all in a state of hyperawareness.

We feel alive because we are truly stretching our human capabilities. When the tension from such intense concentration releases, we are exhausted from having completed hard work, but the results — renewed and expanded visions of ourselves — turn effort into sheer joy.

Know that the experience of conceptualizing will quickly endear itself to you, for this special kind of thinking is not unlike throwing the windows open to let fresh air fill the house of your soul. *So take in a deep breath of fresh air from a place where you have never ever been before.*

THINKING
ALONG
A LINE

A good way to understand the mechanics of linear thinking is to imagine Ford's assembly line once again. An assembly line is a line that figuratively, if not literally, moves in a straight-arrow fashion from point A to point B. After all, the shortest distance between two points is a straight line — provided that the path between A and B is without peaks and valleys.

And so, straight lines will always hold high appeal because their directness represents optimal efficiency. Shorter distance means less time, and less time usually means less cost — thus offering the greatest opportunity for improved profitability. That is, after all, what business managers and owners since Ford's day have been trying to achieve.

The whole notion of the straight line as the preferable path was summarized most adroitly by one of the largest global business consulting firms. A few years ago, one of the firm's advertisements in the *Wall Street Journal* displayed two points on a large blank space, with one dot labeled "A" and the other

"B." Their headline implied that they were adept at providing their clients with straight-line solutions.

124　　At first glance, linear thinking seems like a safe and sure way to avoid failure and increase success. And in some cases — like your standard assembly line — it is. For example, let's say that point A represents the unassembled parts of a TV, and point B represents the fully manufactured unit. What if at point B you discover that the TV won't accept signals from a remote control? All that's needed is to follow each step along the line from point B back to point A, until the point where the assembly procedure broke down can be identified and then fixed. Problem solving could not be more logical — or more efficient.

Linear thinking is grounded in the syntax of language and the mathematics of numbers. The linear world abounds with logic, reason, and analysis. It pays attention to the clock and adheres unwaveringly to pre-established rules. Linear thinking finds errors and corrects them. It dots the "i" and crosses the "t." It makes sure the columns and rows of numbers in a spreadsheet all add up.

Confronted with the "Think different" ad campaign launched by Apple Computer, Inc., which features photographs of revolutionary individuals such as Albert Einstein, Jane Goodall, Frank Sinatra, and Cesar Chavez, someone who is focused on using linear thinking might want to correct the headline "Think different," to read "Think differently."

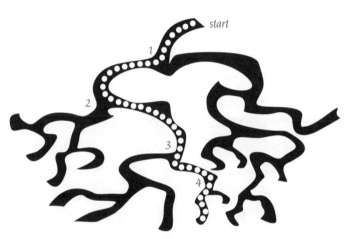

1, 2, 3, *and* 4 *indicate critical junctures*

The most strategic application of linear thinking comes in choosing between alternative courses of action. Such a situation is best described as a critical juncture, where one path needs to be selected from among several forks in the road ahead. The linear method allows for the development of selection criteria that qualify one path from another. Each possible alternative is evaluated according to the qualifying factors, and the final result of each linear analysis is compared to select the best.

If you have heard someone invalidate a decision by saying "you can't compare apples to oranges," they are pointing to the most frequent mistake made using linear thinking. Selection criteria are too often applied one at a time, with one criterion representing each critical juncture. But in this sequential application, once a particular path is chosen, the opportunities along the paths not chosen are forever hidden from view.

In most instances, the linear thought process will only be valid when it systematically weighs all important selection criteria *simultaneously*, rather than in sequence. In this way, opportunities are evaluated equally, thus providing the objectivity necessary for sound decision making. Linear thinking, then, is the best way to solve a problem, to return to a well-defined set of quality standards, or to make valid comparisons. But linear thinking cannot guarantee that a particular vision is optimal. The conceptual input bears this responsibility.

Only *vision* that sees well beyond the confines of paths and critical junctures can uncover alternate courses of action worthy of systematic and simultaneous linear evaluation. It all comes down to a situation of "garbage in - garbage out."

REAL-
LIFE
EXAMPLES

ere are two examples of how linear thinking can be pushed beyond reasonable application in a productivity-based environment.

A local restaurant manager tells its hosts that it is company policy not to seat anyone until their whole party has arrived. The thinking behind this policy is sound. The sooner each dining party orders after being seated, the sooner the table is made available for another party of diners. Profits increase, provided that the restaurant is filled to capacity.

But say you arrive at a time when the dining room is almost completely empty — only six out of 25 tables are occupied. There you stand at the entrance, burdened by a heavy winter coat, umbrella, briefcase, and laptop. Even after you explain that you will need a table for three and the other two people are walking from just one block away, the host proceeds to inform you that you cannot be seated until your entire party is present.

This frustrating turn of events happens when a company issues strict rules governing employee behavior. In this example, the company has effectively suspended the ability of the host to apply a guideline under varying circumstances.

When confronted by a customer who is physically burdened, the most important consideration is making the customer comfortable, instead of adhering strictly to company policy. If the restaurant were filled to capacity, then the company's rule would apply, but with a more-than-half-empty restaurant, the company's rigidity sets the host up for a customer service failure. What's more, it sends a message to employees that they cannot be trusted with even the simplest level of decision making.

This misuse of linear thinking, which employs a single selection criterion — profitability — to establish a strict code of conduct, forgets the potent impact of customer satisfaction on profitability. It's interesting to note that this was an actual experience I had in a restaurant which has since been sold to new owners.

Here's another example. *The Wall Street Journal* (WSJ) one morning featured a front-page article about how an actuarial consulting company advised health care insurers. It seems that much cost could be saved when caring for seniors with cataracts in both eyes if the insurer limited coverage to vision restoration surgery in only *one* eye.

128

What are the values and guidelines behind this kind of reasoning? I can only suspect that the thought process might go something like this: seniors are costing insurers too much, especially now that they live so much longer, and over the course of a longer lifetime they use so many more health care services. The goal is cost containment, even if it means rationing services. And so a linear approach, using sequential logic, can be used to justify what would otherwise seem like an outrageous conclusion.

The WSJ article went on to report that the one-eye-only plan was rejected because of ophthalmologist and patient dissatisfaction.

Whenever we become captivated by the quick fix that the straight line provides, there is the danger that we will bypass the conceptual and fail to anticipate all the factors that influence an outcome.

This is the only genuine potential for failure that we as humans face: the failure to THINK fully and completely, to weave both the conceptual and the linear into a whole.

By corollary, holistic thinking provides our ultimate opportunity in life. If we take advantage of it, each of us can and will be successful at being truly human, truly humane, and truly compassionate.

CREATING THE WHOLE

*A*s our thinking about thinking demonstrates, at some point it is absolutely necessary to dissolve the glue that holds our feet to the ground — so that we can move through the multiple dimensions of space, where quality ideas take shape.

To some extent, each of us already uses conceptual thinking to make sense of our days. But what is now called for are deliberate journeys into the realm of heightened consciousness.

Each of us can purposefully trigger conceptual thinking.

Let's begin with a simple illustration of how you can move from the linear mode to the conceptual. If you use word-processing software, you have probably noticed that such programs are conscientiously designed to call your attention to any word or sentence where the software predicts possible errors. But what happens when you stop to correct the misspelled word or the wrong verb tense? In the process of removing errors, you just might lose the entire gist of your thoughts. Why not allow

your ideas to unfold, regardless of how many technical errors creep into your expression of those
ideas, before applying spelling and grammar
checks? Give the conceptual process of idea generation full reign before invoking the linear thinking
that purges errors.

   In other words, a conceptual journey cannot
begin until you choose to forcibly turn off linear
thinking. Exclude thoughts of details and errors
from your mind. Keep in mind that in an information age, anything you need to know can be accessed
with a simple point and click. So go ahead and give
yourself a break from watching those TV game
shows that are based on the recall of obscure facts. It
is up to you to forcibly chase the words and numbers
out of your mind for at least a while.

**Conceptual thinking requires the child-
like ability to fantasize.**

   Close your eyes, and in this quiet darkness,
begin to really see. Bring to mind an image of something you like, something you find pleasant.

   As you may have surmised, I picture a beach
with shells in my mind's eye whenever I wish to
leave linear methods behind. Because this favorite
image that I visit over and over again is so attractive
and appealing, so full of color, so open and spacious,
words and numbers become unwelcome intruders.

From this starting point I commence my conceptual journeys. All I have to do is let go of the minutia — the *to do* lists — that crowd my days, and surrender to what my mind creates for me to see.

132   It takes practice and time to develop this capability. Because there are no right or wrong outcomes for your journey, and because no one else but you can know its contents, you are always safe. The images you see do not bind you to specific decisions; instead, they feed your imagination, to be molded by your heightened consciousness into solutions, ideas, and strategies.

At first your only goal will be to allow your mind to create visual and spatial images. As children, we are very adept at creating fantasies and daydreams. You can recapture this skill, and invest time in its practice, in order to be well on your way toward creating future vision.

When you become the center of the vision, you will find your truly human self.

With practice, you will begin to deepen the experience by purposefully guiding your visualization. Ultimately, *you* must become the central focus of your journey in order to see your future self.

Imagine drifting in a canoe down a gentle stream. Along the way, on the banks, you see your life re-created — from when you were born to the

present. See your entire life unfold as you drift along. In the canoe, you are an observer, conscious of all that you know about yourself. When you were happiest. When you excelled. When you were in sync with the rhythm of nature. When your gifts and talents flourished. And when your relationships were trusting and authentic. What were you doing at these specific times? Recall how these quality life experiences felt and looked to you.

Purposefully distinguish the satisfying experiences from those that were dissatisfying. Examine these latter ones to identify habits and patterns that need to be broken in order to make way for your future self. With this enhanced awareness of what you know about your entire life, you can then turn your focus to the future.

Regardless of lifestyle and circumstance, we all have this sense of who we are and who we can become. Many times, it takes repeated journeys to peel away the expectations of others and reach our own innate desires and abilities. Allow all your gifts, talents, and traits to flourish to full potential in your mind's eye. See what you are doing five, ten, or twenty or more years from now. What would your day look like when you are at your best, and when your world offers you only continuing challenges to push your capabilities beyond all limits? Imagine how good it would feel to be in this state of being. Use this sensation to motivate yourself to return again and again to this vision.

When this happens, you have reached a future vision of your truly human self. With time and repeated journeys this vision will continue to deepen, but it will never completely come into focus. For if every detail is clear, then linear thinking is taking over and adding unnecessary complexity to a vision that is profoundly beautiful in its simplicity.

Make the vision of your truly human self strategic by using both conceptual idea generation and linear analysis.

How you will achieve your vision is an even greater challenge than the creation of future vision itself. This is because you will need to use both linear and conceptual methods in alternating sequence.

Using a predominantly linear approach, first take on the task of information gathering. Seek to collect all pertinent facts that can affect your vision. Part of this requires that you immerse yourself in your surrounding world to identify the most likely sources of change.

Where will new opportunity occur? Where might threats be hidden? Take in as much of your world as you possibly can, and saturate yourself with this information. Temper this view of the external

world with your understanding of what has worked
well in the past, as well as your urgent short-term ver-
sus long-term needs. Throughout this process you are
a collector, adding what you know from both the
world outside you and the world inside you to define
your situation in life.

135

Now it is time to shift to the conceptual mode
of thinking and live with the chaos created by this
glut of information. Take a conceptual journey, con-
centrating on your vision of your future self. See
what ideas form as your mind puts order to the
chaos by linking and transforming what is known
into something new.

It was through this use of linear information-
gathering on shell architecture, followed by intense
focus on conceptualizing shell images, that I was able
to extrapolate shell growth to human growth and
develop the strategies contained in the *Principles of
Truly Human Growth* presented in Part Six.

In practice, you will find that by following
this method, you will move back and forth between
the linear and conceptual modes of thinking until
the conceptual yields strategies for how you will
achieve your vision. If insights do not readily
occur, provide your mind with stimuli from music,
art, or nature itself. Remove any self-imposed pressure to perform on deadlines, for our mechanized

timekeepers do indeed frustrate and delay the realization of our dreams.

Hopefully, by now you are faced with many ideas, from which to choose the one that offers the greatest likelihood of success — that is, the one which is strategic and follows the path of least risk.

The selection process requires that you return to linear methods, systematically evaluating each potential strategy in light of the *Principles of Truly Human Growth*. The extent to which each strategy upholds these principles becomes a measure of the strategy's value to you.

Most likely, you will want to add evaluation criteria specific to your life circumstances, such as the needs of family members, available financial resources, and any special health considerations. The point is, whatever criteria you develop, you will subject each and every strategy under consideration to each and every criterion. The result is a matrix which looks something like this:

STRATEGY	GROWTH PRINCIPLES	CAREER SUCCESS	FAMILY WELL-BEING	FINANCES	HEALTH
A					
B					
C					

Table header: EVALUATION CRITERIA

All you need to do is enter into each box the effect of the strategy on each criterion. Then stand back and see what this "apples to apples" comparison tells you. Because you have used several criteria in the evaluation process, your assessment of the best strategy reflects a broad-based weighting of all the important factors in your life.

If your evaluation produces a clearly superior strategy, then it is time to move into implementation. If not, return to the conceptual mode to reshape your current strategies into ones with significantly greater value. Once a strategy is selected, what remains is the development of a plan of action.

These, then, are the steps in the strategic visioning process. Try them, but go easy on yourself. Becoming adept in this holistic way of visioning is the work of a lifetime. Be satisfied with the outcome you achieve each time you complete the process, and know that with each new strategic visioning experience, you will come even closer to your truly human self.

BENCHMARKING YOUR PROGRESS

*B*ecause we are self-directing, we can also be self-monitoring. Through continued vigilance, we heighten our awareness of the progress we are achieving toward our future vision. We watch and then evaluate how effective we are in the process of growth. This evaluation allows us to continually improve the process, and to detect potentially harmful variances before serious damage occurs.

So how do we know where we stand at any given point in time along the way? This is especially challenging, as our future vision is not a clearly defined endpoint. Rather, it exists in a state of dynamic evolution, always revealing more to us as we progress further in our growth. In this state of perpetual becoming, a yardstick is useless.

Yes, of course we can measure the attainment of goals — like getting a promotion in the next six months, or buying the house of our dreams before we turn 40. But while helpful in keeping us moving on a reasonable, specific plan of action, these goals underestimate the value of our total

selves. We substitute material indicators for that which is intangible.

What's more significant is a measurement of our life experiences. Earlier, I shared with you the benefits I believe will be ever more present to me in a process of authentic growth. As we progress through the years of our lives, we should see each of these benefits present to an even greater extent.

You can use the benefits I outlined in Part Four to assess your overall progress on a continuing basis. Use these benefits as benchmarks of progress, taking care to measure them at the starting point — right here, right now — before you implement any more actions directed toward change. The following recap of the *Benefits of Truly Human Growth* is provided to help you establish this baseline. Then periodically return to your list and reevaluate your progress. Whenever the presence of these benefits in your life is found to be increasing, you have validation that you are moving forward on an authentic journey of truly human growth.

The Benefits of
TRULY HUMAN GROWTH

Liberation of the SPIRIT

Inheritance of WISDOM

Mid-life Crisis PREVENTION

Optimal HEALTH

A World of OPPORTUNITIES

Evolving CAPABILITIES

Inner STRENGTH

Maximized SUCCESS

Genuine HAPPINESS

Passion for LIFE

Unconditional GENEROSITY

Authentic LOVE

A Legacy of IDEAS

A NEW WAY
TO VIEW
YOUR BRAIN

*R*ecently I went to the Commonwealth Club of California to hear what Dr. Robert Ornstein, the author of *The Right Mind*, had to say about his review of scientific research on the capabilities of the right and left hemispheres of the brain.

When Ornstein mentioned that Robert Louis Stevenson's fictional story of Jekyll and Hyde was a portrayal of how the society of his time viewed the different sides of the brain, I immediately recalled seeing Robert Cuccioli perform this complex role on Broadway. I had watched, transfixed, as Cuccioli transformed himself with lightning speed from the good, upstanding, pure-toned and well-groomed Dr. Jekyll, into the crouching, growling, and perverse-looking Mr. Hyde — Jekyll's evil and violent opposite half who would eventually precipitate their shared demise.

Back and forth, back and forth — the good and evil sides of one man's psyche locked in eternal battle, fixed in an unyielding struggle to the very end of life. Each side seeking a winner-take-all victory, each ultimately a loser, perishing in this unresolvable, no-win situation.

142 In Stevenson's time, it was believed that the left brain was where humanity and reason resided. In other words, the left brain was good, while the right brain was considered less than human, unintelligent, prone to violence, and therefore inherently evil. Dr. Jekyll, the kind, intelligent, and upstanding physician, represented the character's left brain struggling to the death with his inherently evil right brain — represented by his mass-murdering twin, Mr. Hyde. And so, without supporting scientific evidence, it was believed that there was a physical basis to the seeming duality of human nature. Good and evil were both innate, literally wired into the physiology of the human brain.

Scientific evidence of brain functioning eventually replaced this brain model with a point of view that went beyond value judgments of good and evil. It was determined that the left brain was where verbal and mathematical skills reside, while the right brain held creative, musical, and artistic abilities.

But during his presentation, Dr. Ornstein offered a fresh perspective of the brain's hemispheres. According to Ornstein, the right brain could be viewed as responsible for context, or '

spatial relationships — what I have referred to as vision and the big picture. This may very well be where we build the conceptual capabilities that allow us to focus on the meaning and implications of complex, multidimensional issues.

The function of the left hemisphere, on the other hand, he now assigned as text. This is where words and numbers, rules, syntax, and meticulous attention to detail are produced, and perhaps this is where the skills of linear thinking reside.

Ornstein's theory offers crucial insights for our personal growth. For it suggests, as I have mentioned before, that we need to use both sides of the brain adeptly — and to be proficient in both linear and conceptual modes of thinking. Working together, they may create an integrated and holistic approach to life, and thereby expand our humanity.

How much further would we evolve as a society, even as a species, if each of us were to carry out the details of our daily lives in sync with the multidimensional vision of our full human potential? Perhaps a new duality is emerging which can facilitate our human reach for excellence. The synergy of text and context, linear and conceptual, may bring us better quality decisions and ultimately greater quality of life.

REVEALING
THE
PROCESS

What did you perceive as the purpose of the previous chapter? My Jekyll and Hyde theater experience was constructed to provide you with opportunity for a conceptual flight of fantasy. Did you join me on this visual re-creation of the struggle between good and evil? Or did you just read the words on the pages for the technical information presented?

Were you more content to be a passive collector of data? Or were you an active participant in the storyline? Strategic vision, when primed by holistic thinking, transforms us from passive bystanders to active leaders of our lives.

As you may have already figured out, this book was not just written to convey information but to provide you, through its very design, with an experience in holistic thinking. Within the confines of the text, which are by definition linear, I have endeavored to open up my mind to you so that you could begin to see how I move back and forth between linear and conceptual modes of thinking.

Taken as a whole, this book follows an overall path of holistic thinking in order to create an environment in which vision can flourish. While Part One used a conceptual reflection to engage your emotions in recognition of daily life dissatisfaction, Parts Two, Three, and Four were designed to flood you with information from a variety of places and times. I was purposefully creating for you a chaos of information to feed your conceptual abilities. The continuing use of rhetorical questions was intended to draw you actively into the issues presented, so that you would become the central focus.

We then journeyed through a reflection based on the images of gastropod shells. By leaving words behind, I shared with you the visual, multidimensional model I use to challenge myself in hopes of better understanding my own growth toward truly human potential. You too can take advantage of this conceptual journey, forcibly leaving the linear way of thinking behind and using shells as visual stimuli for spatial, conceptual thinking.

Finally, by distilling my growth strategy into the *Principles of Truly Human Growth*, I provided a practical, linear set of guidelines that you could use to systematically assess your ideas for the future. Simultaneous application of all eight growth principles, as well as your unique criteria, to your possible strategies for the future, will identify the one of greatest value or cause you to reconceptualize better strategies.

This was my way of not only describing but also *demonstrating* the transition from linear to conceptual and back. Take time to think about how you think, and you will be able to identify both modes of thought at work inside you. Deliberately encourage both the conceptual and the linear, applying each appropriately to the thinking task at hand.

What more important investment of time can there be than that spent in thinking through how you think? What better way to encourage the growth of your inner self, for your own sake and for the sake of all those you touch in the course of your life?

What's next?

The beginning of the end of this book, and the beginning of your commitment to a lifetime of truly human growth.

PART EIGHT

VISION AS

A WAY

OF LIFE

SEEKERS
OF
TRUTH

*A*t college I was educated as a scientist — a bacteriologist, to be precise. For me, this was a life-changing experience that would forever determine the thinking techniques I would utilize to create and pursue my own life's purpose. In hindsight, this was the best possible preparation I could receive for the rest of my life.

I recognize that the prevailing image of a scientist centers on the use of logic and analysis to test the truth. And yes, science is about experimentation, the measurement of how deliberate changes in environmental variables affect a controlled system. It does, in part, embody unemotional, calculated measurements of behavior — all dependent on linear methods of information gathering and analysis.

This training taught me the discipline, accuracy, and precision of linear experimentation; it brought balance to my natural preference for the conceptual. With time and rigorous practice in the scientific method, I came to value *both* the linear and the conceptual as essential. And with even more time and

experience, I was encouraged to continually seek ways to integrate the linear and conceptual more effectively.

Think about how scientists pursue the truth. First, they saturate their minds with all currently known information about a portion of our world; this is a linear, fact-finding mission. Then, the scientist turns into a creator who hypothesizes, or guesses intelligently, about what might be true. This educated guesstimation requires all the skills of the conceptual. Seeing the hidden meanings and possible linkages behind bits of information allows the emergence of a new vision about how nature works. From there, the scientist uses the linear process of experimentation to test whether this vision, the hypothesis, is true.

Sheer childlike curiosity causes the scientist to keep pursuing the truth, for the truth attracts our human consciousness like a magnet. It affirms us as being alive, as living out our authentic humanity.

For many years now, I have come to see the scientific process and strategic visioning as one and the same. In practice, the scientific process is the only methodology I use in my consulting, and it is the one I have endeavored to share with you here.

But it is very important to note that the scientist is not at all unlike the artist. The scientist blends the conceptual and linear, pushing the limits of human understanding by seeking to discover the truths inherent in creation. Similarly, the artist confronts the reality present in the world, and then re-envisions this truth in provocative ways that cause us to react and create *new* truths. Without a doubt, the artist, like the scientist, must be adept at both the linear and the conceptual modes — and at integrating the two to become a holistic thinker.

150

The artist acts linearly in taking in the world's truths, and in mastering the specific techniques of various artistic media. The transformation of current truth into a new reality, meanwhile, relies on the creative powers inherent in the conceptual.

You and I — indeed, each and every one of us — are scientists and artists, for our entire life purpose centers both on seeking the truth intrinsic to us as humans and individuals, and on sharing the creations of our inner selves with the community of all living things. We have been purposefully prepared for this challenge.

As I have said before, it is not that we are incapable of thinking holistically. Perhaps inexperienced, but not incapable. It is all a matter of what we have become accustomed to doing, and the thinking habits we have fallen into. So no matter whether you have formed a preference for either the linear or the conceptual, know that with specific skills and practice you can become an adept holistic thinker.

A friend of mine, who teaches reading and composition to freshman students at one of the country's top-ranking universities, reports that one of the most difficult skills to convey to his students is the art of revision. He explains that revision, as the word suggests, entails more than just adding a sentence here or there; it means totally *re-envisioning* the argument in a new way. But this proves to be a formidable stumbling-block for most students, and a reflection on the predominantly linear education they have received.

Happy and content to fix technical errors or expand an already-existing thought, these students miss the very human pleasure of engaging in visioning. Fortunately, my friend insists that his students put aside the old document and start anew, in order to take a completely fresh perspective on their work.

For the most part, in our American society, we have not been well-trained in the art of revision. And this, sadly, speaks to a pervasive lack of vision in society itself. For if we are to live as works in progress, always in the process of growing to become more, revising our future vision becomes the center of our life purpose and the existence of the society we choose to create.

THE OPPORTUNITY

*A*re we ready to cross the threshold from our productivity-based industrial age to one that is driven by information?

Today, because of the sacrifices made by Henry Ford's assembly line workers — and all those who followed them — we are in a position of strength from which to undertake this voyage. Their hours of toil came at a personal price: a compromise in independent decision-making. But for the sake of a greater good, together they created the security that we benefit from today. We will be healthier and live longer; we will have the freedom and the money to fill our lives to the brim with comfort, convenience, and recreation, all thanks to their commitment to a better way of life.

But we need to recognize that in the 1930s and 1940s, "security" meant something very different from what we have now. It meant finding food for tomorrow night's supper, making do with last year's clothes. Planning was simple then. No need for day timers and to do lists. Life was about rolling

up your sleeves and doing whatever you could to get by. It was the resourcefulness of the human spirit that allowed so much to be accomplished with so few means during depression and war. That resourcefulness, in the end, was the response of *truly human* human beings to the ebb and flow of circumstances.

Now the situation is reversed. So many resources are at our fingertips, so much information is only a mouse click away. And what are we going to do in this time of plenty?

More of everything translates to much more complexity in our daily lives. We all know this, and we are all feeling, if not reeling from, its effects. This complexity demands more organization and thoughtful planning. In a way, each of us will need to "professionalize" our very approach to living.

No matter what you do, you will — if you don't already — deal in specialized information that you might have been denied access to or that simply did not exist just years ago.

Information will instantly flood your computer screen from innumerable sources. And what about the sources of information? Will it be easy for you to distinguish fact from fiction? Or will we all require new skills to transform this information into the organized knowledge requisite for sound decision making?

Today's and tomorrow's most valued employees and business owners will be those who can use information to reach independent decisions. There will be no time to wait around while someone else makes a decision for you. As a result, those who can envision the big picture will be most valued.

154

Employers now send out pleas for this new breed of so-called *knowledge workers*, realizing that the assembly line workers and supervisors they previously developed are now less than well-prepared for the challenge that unlimited and instantaneous information provides.

The Sunday business section of the *Los Angeles Times* reported, in December, 1995, a successful company turnaround when each worker was allowed to assemble an entire product. One employee making one product start to finish was able to see the whole, and so better at preventing errors. A good idea — or one born too late? Are the visionary leaders of such companies really ahead of their time, or has our mechanized way of doing put us all in a game of catch-up?

No matter what you do or how you earn your living, you will likely be a translator of *information* into organized *knowledge*, which will inspire *actions* that change yourself and the world in which you live. And while this has traditionally been the role of

the professional in our society, we all must now take on professional responsibilities. Each of us will be a decision maker in this brave new world that demands conscious thinking and feeling as an essential component of doing.

What a magnificent wake-up call to heighten awareness of our vast human capacity for consciousness. For this is truly a zenith in human history, a time of boundless opportunity in which to be alive. What better environment for reaching your personal best than when the world depends on what you know, envision, and decide?

And so this current time can be transformed into something much more than an information age, if we decide to achieve more. From this moment forward, we can choose to create an age of authentic professionalism. We can stand together as peers and colleagues, respecting and benefitting from the unique contributions that each of us brings forth to create the whole.

It's now morning, and your alarm clock heralds a new day. So what are you going to do differently? Will you still choose to end your day with unnecessary frustration and dissatisfaction? Or will you take charge of the situation and forcibly introduce the changes that will facilitate your success?

THE
ONE
DECISION

*T*here is one decision that each of us faces.
Heightened consciousness empowers us to
decide whether or not to embark on a deliberate
course toward full human and individual potential.
Our growth is a matter of personal choice.

Some of us will decide to just let life happen,
avoiding change and adhering to the tried and true.
Others of us will commit to using our awareness of
all that we know to take charge of the future. And
those of us who do will move from a reactive to a
proactive position in life, inspired by the vision of all
we are and all we can become.

After all, the risk of living life without really
knowing what can be accomplished is not a viable
alternative. Each of us has the opportunity to fully
embrace growth as a *truly human* human being.
And when we do, we will realize that we have chosen
well, for growth brings security by making us ever
more competent and capable in the business of living.

There are no instincts that you can fall back
on when making this one decision. Stall tactics are

just the same as making a decision not to grow, for in the absence of a decision, the status quo remains.

As far as I'm concerned, I cannot delay, put off, or take any extra time to reach a lasting decision. I find the vision of becoming a *truly human* human being so irresistible that I have no second thoughts about wanting to pursue this as my most central life purpose. This is my spirituality, the way in which I understand my place in creation; it brings me the hope that keeps me moving forward when challenged by changing life circumstances. I see no other viable way to inner peace.

And peace does come in the form of small signs and symbols that affirm your life strategy along the journey. I know this is true from firsthand experience. Recently I located the creative center for the *Truly Human* project in a space formerly occupied by a medical book dealer. There, I was amazed to find that the only non-medical book abandoned among the numerous antiquated ophthalmology texts was a copy of Teilhard de Chardin's *The Phenomenon of Man*. The very words that inspired my original vision were there, waiting for me to discover them once more.

Vision is and always will be as simple and mysterious as this.

157

HOW
VISION
CONFIRMS HOPE

*A*s you continue on your journey, it is essential to remind yourself of this life-changing commitment to growth. Keep a symbol of authentic growth — perhaps a shell left behind by its former owner, or an artist's depiction of a gastropod's architecture — as an integral part of your life. You need not expend resources in preparing this image; a simple line drawing of an outward spiral will do.

Because this is your special image, around which you are formulating your own unique vision, keep it out of sight — tucked away, perhaps in a box or personal treasure chest. Then once each day, visit this symbol of growth. Use it to recall the *Principles of Truly Human Growth*, and focus each day's effort on reaching for your vision instead of filling time with busyness. With practice, it will take no more than a minute or two to align your day's priorities with what really matters.

But do take care not to worship or idolize this form. Keep in mind that all it is, and all it ever needs to be, is a reminder of how nature has embedded

clues to our human growth in its very design. In this way, we can make what might well be overwhelming into a simple, natural way of life.

If you are persistent in allowing yourself to transform your thoughts into wide, expansive dreams of who you can become, you will effectively bring yourself into a new realm of living based on the most important value of all. And that is hope.

For with vision, you will realign your view of yourself so that you are convinced of your innate ability to grow through each challenge that life pro- vides. Believing this, you will find that the world can never be a place of hopelessness or despair.

With vision, we realize that we can use the power and wisdom of consciousness strategically, deliberately planning each action so as to be most effective and successful. Not only do we live from a solid base of security and comfort, but with vision, everything we do becomes part of a purposeful whole. And the vision of our truly human selves, projected out into the future, is so compelling, so thoroughly irresistible, that all we can do is pursue it with all our might.

No matter how often we may feel frustrated or stymied along the way, no matter how many times others interrupt our actions and bring momen- tary pause to our intended plans, no matter how angry or sad we might have previously been, there is no longer any room for fear.

For hopelessness, frustration, and fear all flourish in those who will not envision how much better things can be. Such self-defeating notions are fed by time-cramming, by filling days to overflowing and thereby effectively excluding any opportunity to think about life's ultimate purpose.

But the hope vision brings sends dissatisfaction and frustration packing once and for all. I know this because I have experienced this change in my own life. My days now fit into a better whole, and there is significantly less reliance on coping mechanisms to reduce the eventual buildup of stress.

Know that you too can do this for yourself. It's all just a matter of finding and then wholeheartedly believing in your vision. For this is the ultimate pursuit of truth, *your truth,* and how this truth becomes inextricably linked to the truth in all of creation. Take pride and deep satisfaction in the development of the glorious gifts that you have been given. Then see how this truth will set you free of the clock's gargantuan hands. And by experiencing day after hope-filled day, the days of your life will find lasting peace.

PART NINE

THE

AUTHOR'S

AFTERWORD

TRIAL BY FIRE

Thanksgiving weekend, 1998.

Just before leaving for this year's annual family gathering in the Napa Valley wine country, I found myself pausing to look at my grandmother Irene's wedding photograph. I couldn't help but recall how many times, as a child, I would prepare on this very same day to leave with my parents for her warm, simple flat in San Francisco's Marina District.

Irene and Jack Bacigalupi's home was always the gathering place for family on Thanksgiving — a home where food never seemed to stop flowing from the kitchen. But somewhere between cooking and serving copious amounts of Italian antipasti, ravioli, and American turkey with stuffing, my grandmother would retell her remembrances of the devastating 1906 San Francisco Earthquake and ensuing fire.

Even though she was just a young girl living with her parents, brothers, and sister on Telegraph Hill in the center of North Beach when the earthquake struck, that moment and the days that followed were as vivid to her in her 50s, 60s, 70s, and

80s as when she was merely nine years old. And so, year after year, the story was retold.

Beginning with how the fire destroyed the family home on Stockton Street, she would always recite the same set of details. My grandmother, along with her parents and siblings, were evacuated to safety from the advancing fire line by the U. S. Army. Spending many weeks in Golden Gate Park, sleeping in makeshift tents, they received food from kindhearted nuns with long, flowing habits and flying white headdresses.

Irene's father, P. G. Molinari, who had a fledgling salami factory and delicatessen, was left with virtually no resources — except for the Parmesan cheese and olive oil he had hastily salvaged and buried in a vacant lot. But with a loan given on a handshake from North Beach friend A. P. Giannini — founder of the Bank of Italy, which became Bank of America — he began, without hesitation, the task of rebuilding his family's life and livelihood. Soon a new home was constructed on Greenwich Street directly behind Sts. Peter and Paul Church. My great-grandfather's business, P. G. Molinari & Sons, revived and grew so steadily that it continues to thrive to this very day.

This story was no doubt a compelling reason for our family to give special thanks each Thanksgiving. And it was there, during those warm family celebrations, that my grandmother would unknowingly prepare me for my future.

On the night of October 18, 1991, I set out on a trip to St. Thomas at the invitation of my good friend Jean Caramatti. The ostensible purpose was vacation, sun, shopping, and a break from the responsibilities of consulting.

But I also held a deeper justification and purpose in mind. By distancing myself from my current daily life, I would have the physical and emotional space necessary for planning how to get started on my next phase of personal growth. Amidst St. Thomas' slower and warmer lifestyle, I set out to think in an open and creative way about the vision I held for my future, which I knew would hinge on becoming an author.

Not that the act of writing itself was my passion; rather, my life vision was based on the premise that whatever I learn of value from all my experiences should be shared. If my legacy of thoughts, observations, and conclusions helps others to better find their dreams in our world of mechanized living, then my life has achieved its purpose. And so books became an integral part of this vision.

But what happened next would affect the content of my first book — this book — irrevocably.

On Sunday afternoon, two days after my arrival, a phone call greeted me just as I returned to my hotel room after a pleasant drive to the other side of the island. A member of my firm's staff was calling to let me know that she had just heard news reports of a fire moving through the Oakland hills. She had no way of knowing if this fire would be a threat to my house, but thought it best to alert me.

For the next several hours I phoned repeatedly — first to my home, where all I heard was a busy signal, and then to nearby friends, only to receive the same dead-end response. I extended calls to friends and family in cities a good fifteen miles away from where I lived before I could locate a ringing phone and reach someone with information.

Over the next several hours, I learned how, on that hot, windy day, the sky had instantly turned black just after noontime. My home, my car, cherished family mementos, and most importantly my dear cat Cocolat, had all been reduced to a simple, shapeless pile of white ash by the 2000-degree inferno.

I only share this with you because I believe if you can understand my personal insights following the devastation of the Oakland Firestorm, which ravaged over 1800 acres of hillside terrain — claiming nearly 3000 homes and apartments — you may come to an even better understanding of the message of this book. That is, how a strategic view of the future can make for security and growth in the midst of the change, and even disasters, that life presents to us.

When final word was received in St. Thomas that all had indeed perished, I remember letting out a small scream — almost because I thought I should react that way. I clearly remember crying, even shaking, but being so well supported by my friend Jean. But there was another reaction experienced simultaneously with this grief — one of both surrender and a new unfathomable freedom.

On the one hand, I was now faced with the energy-exhausting process of putting the material side of my life back together, which would delay for years the realization of my book project. At the same time, I was intrigued by my brief glimpse of how beautiful life can be when it is freed of the typical burdens and obligations of daily living.

It is the freedom of surrender to life's circumstances, not the energy drain, that remains with me most clearly to this day. This is the feeling I seek to repeat and hopefully understand most fully at my inevitable moment of physical death.

From the very first reports, my parents, family, and friends were all so very supportive. But there was one thing I needed to do all by myself when I returned to Oakland, and that was to visit my plot of

ground. Up until then, the entire experience remained in good part unreal to me, even though I had already seen the news accounts on CNN — and the remnants of my home depicted as a small rectangular splotch at the very center of *Time* magazine's two-page photo of the damage. But these images could not prepare me for what I saw once I stood alone amidst the ashes. Total devastation was in every direction I looked. Only a very few crumbling chimneys were left, accompanied by the eerie, black, denuded trunks of pine trees.

I had brought a bouquet of yellow roses with me, and placed it where my bed once stood — knowing that this is where my cat would most likely have hidden before succumbing to the smoke. Next I moved to the area that was to the right of my bed, where inside a chest, I kept one of my most valued possessions. I dug into the layers of white ash using a trowel and recovered a now-deformed crucifix that had been on my grandmother Irene's casket. Her platinum wedding rings were also retrieved, embedded deeply into a black charred mass. Two tiny blue and white Imari dishes and a few small, discolored, faded china cups were all that remained.

I left that visit with an especially hollow feeling, knowing that a few doors away, a teenage girl perished, unable to escape the fire's swift advance.

While that emptiness will remain with me all the days of my life, I soon learned there was need to limit my grief to small episodes, which I found eventually decreased in frequency. I returned to my office right away and put all energy possible into bringing my life back to order. My consulting commitments had to be fulfilled, and a new house had to be found and made into a home. But throughout it all, one thing remained constant; the future vision I had carried to St. Thomas was always with me, urging me forward. And that, more than anything else, eased the pain and filled me with hope and determination in the midst of crisis.

Though it took a few years, once my life returned more or less to what it had been prior to the fire, I knew it was time to put my vision into action. As I moved purposefully toward planning how to transform my life, I discovered that I was much less distracted by trivia and concerns over unnecessary risk. As a result, I made decisions from a secure new perspective of having plenty of time. No more rushing to artificial finish lines that divide winners from losers.

I recognize now that I cannot push an idea through before its time. Rather, I enjoy the incubation process; getting there, instead of being there, is what matters. Quality isn't instant — so I am

168

mindful that the quick fix never really fixes. Time is more and more a friend than an enemy, a reassuring rhythm that guarantees my life will be filled with variety, questions, decisions, change, and challenge.

I can't ask for anything more from life than this. For it is in my response to the fluctuating circumstances of daily life that I can find and form my truly human self.

The strength of my confidence hit home one day not long after the fire, when I went to purchase some basics that needed to be replaced. The store was very gracious, and offered a welcome discount to shoppers who lost clothes and household items in the fire. But when I made my first purchases, I quickly found that each salesperson wrote the words "fire victim" on our receipts.

I never said a word to anyone at the store, but deep down inside I was repulsed at the notion of being thought of as a victim. For the loss of material possessions in no way compromised me as a human being. I was just as capable and just as committed as before. Nothing of real substance had changed, except that I understood and felt life more deeply as a result of the fire experience — and am now even more focused on what I see as my future.

My grandmother's annual storytelling had indeed prepared me to react this way. "Victim" was never in her vocabulary. And so it wasn't in mine. Her retelling of an equally powerful, life-changing event was never about what things were lost, only about the importance of being with those she loved. I had love and support from my parents, family, and friends in my life before, during, and after the fire. And that was and always will be all that matters.

170

I also believe the fire became kindling for a more insightful book than I would have written if my life had proceeded uninterrupted. For then, I would have focused narrowly on issues affecting business, and never gotten to the heart of what really matters — an understanding of how each of us can purposefully grow toward our future vision.

So was the fire bad or good, destructive or constructive? It was none of these. For it was simply a challenge for me to explore the good and the constructive that already existed within.

Helpless, dependent, insecure, and fearful is no way to live. And if I told you I know from first-hand experience that a vision of authentic growth can make you capable, independent, secure, and fearless, how much of your time and energy would you devote to making your vision a reality? Join with me as we continue throughout our lives to seek out the ultimate meaning of being *truly human.*

Photo by: Pete Carmichael

If I *am truly human,*
I will search 'til I find the gifts I have inside.
And if I *am truly, truly human,*
I *may lose my way*
but trust my heart will lead me back again.

— Johnathan Dax
Composer
Truly Human Theme Song

$\mathcal{A}$CKNOWLEDGEMENTS

To all the truly human people who have supported me throughout my life, especially my parents, family, and friends. In particular, I wish to acknowledge the many hours of listening, creative support, and love given to me throughout the development of this new model for human growth by Jean Caramatti, Joseph Connell, Winifred Kostainsek, Sergio Apodaca, and Adrienne Gilmore.

To Clara Kim, Geraldine Poon, and Nilmini Gunaratne, who taught me much about the serious challenges they faced in forming effective careers centered on lifelong values, while I advised them as students in the Prytanean Women's Honor Society at the University of California, Berkeley.

To UCB Ph.D. candidate in literature Gary Schmidt; to artists Sarah Jane Charubin and Bill Goff; to photographers Pete Carmichael and Judy Houston; and to my printer Pete Murai at Madison Street Press, who have all helped this book come into physical being.

And most importantly, I must express my deepest and most heartfelt love and gratitude to Lenora Nori Shishido, Executive Director of Umano. Nori, let us always be fully present to each other as we bring forward this exciting message of human growth in all the years that lie ahead.

And finally to each of you, my readers. While I may not yet know you personally, we now share a common bond of information and human understanding that will hopefully become an essential part of the legacy we leave to those who follow us.

172

UMANO

Dear Readers:

In Italian, *umano* means human, humane, and compassionate. This definition is the essence of our organization's vision. Celebrating humanity, grace, and the well-being of mind, body, and soul through books, music, seminars, and theatrical and multimedia productions, UMANO aims to serve you with the highest level of integrity and purpose.

UMANO was founded by Barbara Bacigalupi to foster holistic thinking, and to further the paradigm shift in heightened human consciousness portrayed by this book. Our shared mission is to create the necessary dialogue between individuals from all ages and origins as they seek to define for themselves what it means to be truly human. Our service extends to businesses and organizations that aspire to these values. We hold as our ultimate goal the widespread incorporation of holistic thinking practices into public and private educational systems.

We hope that UMANO will become the one place for all your truly human needs. We look forward to having you share your ideas and interests with us, and to serving you now and through the years to come.

Very truly yours,

Lenora Shishido
Executive Director

BARBARA BACIGALUPI

Audiobook

174 *Truly Human* is available as an audiobook, read by the author and musical theater star Christopher Carl.

Guided Imagery Meditations

These audiotapes and CDs are designed to promote relaxation and build skills in conceptual thinking and visioning.

Keynote Addresses and Workshops

Barbara Bacigalupi and other UMANO speakers are available for conventions, businesses, and associations. A multimedia presentation style, which incorporates visual imagery, music, demonstrations, and movement, is a hallmark of UMANO. Programs can be customized to center on those specific issues that are important to your organization.

Attention Teachers

A guide is available for faculty discussions of *Truly Human* and its implications for effective education. At the UMANO web site, there is a special place for you to share your opinions and ideas with other educators.

For more information,
to place an order, or to join our mailing list:

Order Online:	www.umano.com
E-Mail:	info@umano.com
Fax:	415.989.9854
Mail:	442 Post St., 2nd Floor San Francisco, CA 94102

The one place to find
everything Truly Human online...

www.umano.com

LEARN

how to deepen your
life experiences with
Truly Human.

SEE

the photos from
the shell essay
in full color.

BEGIN

to practice skills in holistic
thinking with special
online exercises.

TOUR

Barbara's learning center,
where she will show you her
sources of inspiration.

SHARE

your personal strategic
vision and stories of truly
human achievement.

INTERACT

by asking the author
questions about
Truly Human.

LISTEN

to clips from audiobooks,
music CDs, and guided
imagery meditation tapes.

SHOP

for books, audiotapes,
CDs, art, and gifts at
our secure online store.

BECOME

a regular member of the
Truly Human online
community.

Truly Human - the Music

This entertaining and provocative collection of songs, arranged in
creative, contemporary pop and light jazz, is sung by two of
musical theater's brightest stars — Christopher Carl, who is best
known for his nearly four-year stint as Raoul in *The Phantom of*

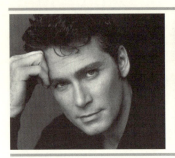

Photos by: Russell Baer

Christopher Carl   Brian Lane Green

the Opera, and Tony-nominated Broadway actor and vocalist
Brian Lane Green. This CD includes a booklet filled with photos and personal messages from Barbara, describing why she
selected each of these songs for your listening pleasure.

Here is a sampling of the songs included:

- **Truly Human** - the title song, premiering the musical composition of Seattle songwriter Johnathan Dax.

- **The Music of the Night** - as it has never been recorded, weaving
  voice and acoustic guitar together seamlessly.

- **A New Life** and **This is the Moment** - from the popular
  musical theater production of *Jekyll & Hyde*.

- **Dreamscape** - from multiple Academy Award-winning songwriter Stephen Schwartz.

- **Something's Coming** - a Leonard Bernstein and
  Steven Sondheim classic, now pairing voice with percussion.

- **Dream** - written by jazz recording artist Patti Cathcart Andress of
  Tuck & Patti.

- **Seasons of Love** - the rousing anthem from the second act of
  Jonathan Larson's *RENT*.

Visit *www.umano.com* for sound clips of this original music.
Produced by Barbara Bacigalupi and Steve Savage.

$\mathcal{A}$BOUT
THE
$\mathcal{A}$UTHOR

$\mathcal{B}$arbara Bacigalupi graduated Phi Beta Kappa with bachelor's and master's degrees earned in microbiology from the University of California, Berkeley. Fascinated by the dynamics of organizations, she dedicated her career to the application of the scientific method to business decision making.

As part of a major hospital's management team, Barbara focused on the complexities of health care and patient service relationships. Then, in 1985, she established her own national firm, Bacigalupi Associates, becoming one of a very few planning and marketing consultants to specialize in the professions. Building experience in both the for-profit and not-for-profit sectors, she pioneered an innovative planning process called Decision Point. Based on the use of opinion data, all members of an organization's constituency can use this methodology to participate in the creation of future direction.

In 1992, Barbara launched the Legacy Project, which monitors parent and student opinions regarding the effectiveness of private schools. The extensive scope of this study addresses the components of quality education, in order to support educators in the holistic instruction of students.

As a public speaker, Barbara is recognized for her ability to translate complex conceptual material into messages that are meaningful for professional and lay audiences alike.

Barbara Bacigalupi is a third-generation descendant of Italian immigrants who came to the San Francisco Bay Area more than 100 years ago. She currently resides in Northern California.

Photo by: Judy Houston

Barbara Bacigalupi
Strategic Planning Consultant